THE FAMILY
GUIDE TO
PREVENTING
ELDER ABUSE

THE FAMILY GUIDE TO PREVENTING ELDER ABUSE

HOW TO PROTECT YOUR PARENTS—AND YOURSELF

THOMAS LEE WRIGHT

Skyhorse Publishing

Skyhorse Publishing books may be purchased in bulk at special discounts for sales promotion, corporate gifts, fund-raising, or educational purposes. Special editions can also be created to specifications. For details, contact the Special Sales Department, Skyhorse Publishing, 307 West 36th Street, 11th Floor, New York, NY 10018 or info@ skyhorsepublishing.com.

Skyhorse® and Skyhorse Publishing® are registered trademarks of Skyhorse Publishing, Inc.®, a Delaware corporation.

Visit our website at www.skyhorsepublishing.com.

10 9 8 7 6 5 4 3 2 1

Library of Congress Cataloging-in-Publication Data is available on file.

Cover design by Rain Saukas
Cover photo credit by iStock

Print ISBN: 978-1-5107-1648-3
Ebook ISBN: 978-1-5107-1650-6

Printed in the United States of America

This book is dedicated to
Thomas C. Wright,
educator, publisher, philanthropist,
loving son, brother, husband, father and grandfather.

Contents

Introduction

Millions of good people care for vulnerable family members every day, performing the basic thankless tasks of providing support to others with patience and kindness. Compassionate caretakers—whether faithful relatives or healthcare professionals—deserve our respect and praise, as well as our gratitude, because they exemplify the best cultural values of our society.

Unfortunately, there are also those walking among us who prey upon the weak and disabled. These depraved souls, though smaller in number, seemingly operate without qualms of conscience, posing a clear and present danger to those we love. This book explores their malignant methods in order to expose their predatory behavior along with its disastrous consequences.

In the age of the Internet, we know that the ever-shifting sands of social justice demand a constant monitoring of the complex evolving topic of elder abuse. Our goal is to be accessible rather than definitive, and we hope these chapters spur the reader on to further study.

Two modern phenomena have become very troubling in this new century and deserving of your attention beyond the scope of these pages because they make the vulnerable elderly particularly susceptible to being abused.

First, there is an ever-increasing number of patients with progressive neurological disorders among our elderly. As of this writing, there are over five million people afflicted with dementia or Alzheimer's disease in the United States—a number projected to triple to fifteen million by 2050. It is the sixth leading cause of death in America and there is no cure in sight for more than a thousand patients who are diagnosed with this type of affliction each day.

Second, since the onset of the twenty-first century, more and more elderly adults are being forced into guardianships whereby they lose virtually all of their constitutional rights, surrendering control of their health, real estate, and life savings to a court-appointed guardian. By some estimates, more than 1.5 million adults are now in guardianship nationwide (with one hundred thousand more added each year) causing some $30 billion to pass into the control of third parties annually. These numbers are only estimates because there is currently no federal oversight of the guardianship industry in the United States to provide a reliable overview and definitive numbers. This is beyond unfortunate—it is a national disgrace. Our elected legislators must address this crisis of accountability if we truly want to keep track of the fate of our elders.

In this book, we hope to provide you with enough pragmatic advice that you will be able to protect your parents and yourself from these and other harmful trends now afflicting our modern society.

In Part 1, we define elder abuse in its various manifestations. It always begins with isolation. When a vulnerable elder is alone, bad things can happen.

Chapters 1 and 2 define how isolation often comes about—sometimes due to circumstance (illness, bereavement, moving residences etc.), sometimes by intervention of an exploitive third-party ("friend," relative, lawyer, guardian, etc.) bearing eerie similarities to actual kidnapping.

In Chapter 3, we see why it's difficult to prosecute financial crimes perpetrated against the elderly and how to identify and protect a potential victim. Chapter 4 recommends steps to take in preparing an estate plan and planning for long-term illness. Chapter 5 summarizes the top 10 fraud scams used to ambush elderly citizens nationwide, according to the United States Senate Committee on Aging.

Part 2 outlines how you can take real action on behalf of your loved ones. Through vigilance and preparation, it is possible to prevent elder abuse. Chapter 6 tells you what to do if you suspect abuse is taking place. Chapter 7 outlines some important considerations when collaborating with a professional, such as a doctor or lawyer, and discusses their ethical duties and responsibilities. Chapter 8 warns about abusive guardianships and how to avoid them. Strategies and complaint procedures are detailed in chapter 9 should you wish to seek justice for your loved one in the future.

Part 3 shows you how to be proactive in carrying out the wishes of your parent. In Chapter 10, a professional cinematographer issues instructions on how best to record your parent's desires. In Chapter 11, a noted journalist gives advice on how to get your personal story told through the media. Chapter 12 offers advice to caretakers about how to care for themselves and also provides guidance to families in selecting the right retirement community for an aging parent. Chapter 13 lays out a vision for the future from a leader of the annual White House Council on Aging. The final chapter of the book offers a checklist for summarizing all the actions that you will ideally want to take on behalf of your parents.

In the interest of full disclosure, my motivation for writing this book was the victimization of my father by a "friend" who isolated him from his family during his final year of life before passing away at the age of 82. Even now, there's much I wish I would have known and done differently in order to protect him. Hopefully, this book will prove instructive, serving as a modest tribute to my father's work as an educator and philanthropist whose mission was ever and always to alleviate the suffering of others through a legacy of shared knowledge.

In the end and from the beginning, the purpose of this book is to provide a blueprint for learning how to protect our parents. Ultimately, the best defense against elder abuse is the proximity of family—physically and emotionally.

Thomas Lee Wright
Seattle, Washington

What is Elder Abuse?

The Problem

Elder abuse *"includes physical, sexual, or psychological abuse, as well as neglect, abandonment, and financial exploitation of an older person by another person or entity, that occurs in any setting (e.g., home, community, or facility), either in a relationship where there is an expectation of trust and/or when an older person is targeted based on age or disability." (from "Elder Justice Roadmap," funded by the US Department of Justice with support from the Department of Health and Human Services)*

In other words, any older adult, in any family, may experience elder abuse. Sometimes individuals bear responsibility for the abuse. Sometimes broken or ineffective systems and entities bear responsibility. Much more research is needed, but existing data indicate that:

- One out of every ten people aged sixty and older who live at home suffers abuse, neglect, or exploitation.
- In several small studies, about half of people with dementia suffered from abuse or neglect.
- Cognitive impairment reduces financial capacity, increasing risk of financial exploitation.

- High rates of neglect, poor care, or preventable adverse events persist in nursing homes and other long-term care settings where more than two million people (most of them elderly) live.
- About two-thirds of elder abuse victims are women.
- African American, Latino, poor, and isolated older adults are disproportionately victimized.
- For every one case of elder abuse that comes to light, another twenty-three remain hidden.

The Human and Economic Toll

Elder abuse triggers downward spirals for many victims, eroding their health, financial stability, and well-being. It also causes untold suffering for millions of people of all ages. That suffering, in turn, needlessly depletes scarce resources of individuals, families, businesses, charities, and public programs (like Medicare and Medicaid). Research is beginning to illuminate the huge cost of elder abuse:

- Elder abuse triples the risk of premature death and causes unnecessary illness, injury, and suffering.
- Victims of elder abuse are four times more likely to be admitted to a nursing home and three times more likely to be admitted to a hospital.
- Understaffing at nursing homes leads to a 22% increase in unnecessary hospitalizations.
- Most adverse events in nursing homes—due largely to inadequate treatment, care, and understaffing—lead to preventable harm and $2.8 billion per year in Medicare hospital costs alone (excluding additional—and substantial—Medicaid costs caused by the same events).
- Financial exploitation causes large economic losses for businesses, families, elders, and government programs, and increases reliance

on federal health care programs such as Medicaid. Research indicates that those with cognitive incapacities suffer 100% greater economic losses than those without such incapacities.

- One study of older women found that verbal abuse leads to greater declines in mental health than physical abuse only.
- Elder abuse causes victims to be more dependent on caregivers. As a result of providing care, caregivers experience declines in their own physical and mental health and their financial security suffers. The cumulative toll of elder abuse has not yet been quantified but is estimated to afflict more than five million people and costs many billions of dollars a year. Emerging evidence indicates that prevention could save lives and prevent illness, injury, and suffering, while also yielding major cost savings.

Challenges in Responding

In communities across the country, diverse multidisciplinary groups of people trying to address elder abuse in their professional and personal lives are working together to find ways to prevent and respond to the problem. States are grappling with enacting appropriate laws and creating programs, roles for responders, and sanctions for abusers. These efforts are largely uncoordinated, lack sufficient resources, and are uninformed by existing data, program models, and federal standards.

Elder abuse is not an easy problem to address: It can manifest itself in many ways—an older parent isolated and neglected by an adult child or caregiver; domestic violence by a partner (long-term or new); sexual assault by a stranger; abuse or neglect by a partner with advancing dementia; financial exploitation by a trusted family member or professional; or systemic neglect by a long-term care provider that hires too few staff members, provides insufficient training to its staff, and expends too few resources on resident care.

As a result, elder abuse requires responses that take an array of factors into consideration: Norms can vary by racial, ethnic, and religious identity (such as relating to caregiving and money) that can shape the context of elder abuse. Shame, fear, love, loyalty, pride, and a desire to remain independent often influence the decisions of older people at risk. Cognitive incapacity and isolation are accompanied by high rates of elder abuse, and also can influence the decision-making of older adults and their ability to access and participate in services. Adult Protective Services (APS) workers report that mental health and substance abuse issues often are present among perpetrators, victims, or both. Thus, effective prevention, investigation, and intervention require cultural competency and sensitivity to a broad array of issues. In addition, one of the greatest challenges in addressing elder abuse is navigating the right balance among autonomy, safety, and privacy goals.

In short, elder abuse does not fit a single profile. It is a complex cluster of distinct but related phenomena involving health, legal, social service, financial, public safety, aging, disability, protective services, victim services, aging services, policy, research, education, and human rights issues. It therefore requires a coordinated multidisciplinary, multi-agency, and multisystem response. Yet, as noted by the Government Accountability Office in 2011, services, education, policy, and research are fragmented and under-resourced. These challenges have been magnified by the lack of a coordinated strategic agenda. To address that gap, an "Elder Justice Roadmap" initiative funded by the US Department of Justice, with support from the Department of Health and Human Services, has been published that provides some guidance, and we refer to it here.

Elder Abuse is a Problem with Solutions

This roadmap seeks to forge a path to solutions with an informed, coordinated public and private effort at the local, state, and national levels. It offers opportunities for engagement by numerous constituencies—the public, state and local officials, professionals who routinely address elder abuse, allied professionals in related fields, policy makers, educators, researchers, caregivers, others who work to reduce elder abuse, and older adults themselves. It is time not only to identify the problems, but also to expand our knowledge about successful strategies and implement common sense, cost-effective solutions to stem this rising epidemic of elder abuse.

Communities have different needs and resources when it comes to addressing elder abuse. The priorities identified provide ample opportunity for organizations, practitioners, and other interested individuals and entities to participate in tackling aspects of the problem that are most relevant to them. No single entity can address elder abuse by itself. Everyone can make a difference.

PART 1

ELDER ABUSE

Chapter 1

Twenty Facts about Senior Isolation

by Sarah Jamila Stevenson

Sarah Jamila Stevenson is a writer, artist, editor, and graphic designer in Northern California. For over two years, she was a freelance writer for A Place for Mom's *Senior Living blog and "Twenty Facts About Senior Isolation" was first published there during that time. She is also the author of three young adult novels:* The Latte Rebellion, Underneath, *and* The Truth Against the World. *Her first novel for young adults,* The Latte Rebellion, *was a Scholastic Book Club pick as well as an IPPY Bronze Medalist in Multicultural Children's Fiction. Her work has been featured on Capital Public Radio's* Insight *and NPR's* Tell Me More with Michel Martin.

Feelings of loneliness and isolation can lead to serious consequences for senior health. Understanding the causes and risk factors for senior isolation can help us prevent it.

Nobody relishes the prospect of aging without a spouse or family member at their side, without friends to help them laugh at the ridiculous parts and support them through the difficult times. Yet that is just what many North American seniors face. As the baby boomer generation crosses the over-65 threshold, it grows; but many of our aging loved ones are still feeling alone in the crowd.

Statistics on Senior Isolation

According to the US Census Bureau, 11 million people, or 28% of those aged 65 and older, lived alone in 2010. As people get older, their likelihood of living alone only increases. Additionally, more and more older adults do not have children, reports AARP, and that means fewer family members to provide company and care as those adults become seniors.

While living alone does not inevitably lead to social isolation, it is certainly a predisposing factor. Yet another important consideration is how often seniors engage in social activities.

Social contacts tend to decrease as we age for a variety of reasons, including retirement, the death of friends and family, or lack of mobility. Regardless of the causes of senior isolation, the consequences can be alarming and even harmful. Even perceived social isolation—the feeling that you are lonely—is a struggle for many older people. Fortunately, the past couple of decades have seen increasing research into the risks, causes, and prevention of loneliness in seniors. Here are 20 facts about senior isolation to help you stay informed:

1. Senior isolation increases the risk of mortality.

According to a 2012 study in the Proceedings of the National Academy of Sciences (PNAS), both social isolation and loneliness are associated with a higher risk of mortality in adults aged 52 and older.

One possible explanation: "People who live alone or lack social contacts may be at increased risk of death if acute symptoms develop, because there is less of a network of confidantes to prompt medical attention." Efforts to reduce isolation are the key to addressing the issue of mortality, said the study's authors.

2. Feelings of loneliness can negatively affect both physical and mental health.

Regardless of the facts of a person's isolation, seniors who feel lonely and isolated are more likely to report also having poor physical or mental health, as reported in a 2009 study using data from the National Social Life, Health, and Aging Project.

Connecting seniors with social resources, such as senior centers and meal delivery programs, is one way to combat subjective feelings of isolation.

3. Perceived loneliness contributes to cognitive decline and risk of dementia.

Dr. John Cacioppo, a neuroscientist and psychologist at the University of Chicago, has been studying social isolation for 30 years. One frightening finding is that feelings of loneliness are linked to poor cognitive performance and quicker cognitive decline.

We evolved to be a social species, says Dr. Cacioppo—it's hardwired into our brains, and when we don't meet that need, it can have physical and neurological effects.

4. Social isolation makes seniors more vulnerable to elder abuse.

Many studies show a connection between social isolation and higher rates of elder abuse, reports the National Center on Elder Abuse. Researchers are not sure whether this is because isolated adults are more likely to fall victim to abuse, or a result of abusers attempting to isolate the elders from others to minimize risk of discovery.

A critical strategy for reducing elder abuse is speaking up: abuse, neglect, and exploitation often go unreported. As for prevention, maintaining connections with senior loved ones helps ensure their safety.

5. LGBT seniors are much more likely to be socially isolated.

LGBT seniors are twice as likely to live alone, according to SAGE (Services & Advocacy for GLBT Elders); they are more likely to be single and they are less likely to have children—and they are more likely to be estranged from their biological families.

Stigma and discrimination are major roadblocks to support for LGBT seniors, but there are more and more community groups and online resources devoted to helping these elders avoid isolation.

6. Social isolation in seniors is linked to long-term illness.

In the PNAS study mentioned in point #1, illnesses and conditions such as chronic lung disease, arthritis, impaired mobility, and depression were associated with social isolation. Ensuring appropriate care for our loved ones' illnesses can help prevent this isolation. For homebound seniors, phone calls and visits can be a critical part of connecting with loved ones. Others may find that moving to an assisted living community addresses both issues—the need for ongoing care and the desire for companionship.

7. Loneliness in seniors is a major risk factor for depression.

Numerous studies over the past decade have shown that feeling loneliness is associated with more depressive symptoms in both middle-aged and older adults.

One important first step is recognizing those feelings of loneliness, isolation, and depression and seeking treatment—whether it's on your own behalf or for the sake of a loved one.

8. Loneliness causes high blood pressure.

A 2010 study in *Psychology and Aging* indicated a direct relationship between loneliness in older adults and increases in systolic blood pressure over a four-year period. These increases were independent of race, ethnicity, gender, and other possible contributing factors. Early interventions for loneliness, say the study's authors, may be key to preventing both the isolation and associated health risks.

9. Socially isolated seniors are more pessimistic about the future.

According to the National Council on Aging (NCOA), socially isolated seniors are more likely to predict their quality of life will get worse over the next five to ten years, are more concerned about needing help from community programs as they get older, and are more likely to express concerns about aging.

The National Association of Area Agencies on Aging (n4a) says community-based programs and services are critical in helping ward off potential problems and improving quality of life for older people.

10. Physical and geographic isolation often leads to social isolation.

"One in six seniors living alone in the United States faces physical, cultural, and/or geographical barriers that isolate them from their peers and communities," reports the National Council on Aging. "This isolation can prevent them from receiving benefits and services that can improve their economic security and their ability to live healthy, independent lives." Referring isolated older adults to senior centers, activity programs, and transportation services can go a long way toward creating valuable connections and reducing isolation.

11. Isolated seniors are more likely to need long-term care.

Loneliness and social isolation are major predictors of seniors utilizing home care, as well as entering nursing homes. A positive aspect of care in a communal facility is that using long-term health care services can in itself connect seniors with much-needed support. Particularly for seniors in rural areas, entering a care facility may provide companionship and social contact.

12. Loss of a spouse is a major risk factor for loneliness and isolation.

Losing a spouse, an event which becomes more common as people enter older age, has been shown by numerous studies to increase seniors' vulnerability to emotional and social isolation. Besides the loneliness brought on by bereavement, the loss of a partner may also mean the loss of social interactions that were facilitated by being part of a couple.

Ensuring seniors have access to family and friendship support can help alleviate this loneliness.

13. Transportation challenges can lead to social isolation.

According to the AARP, "life expectancy exceeds safe driving expectancy after age 70 by about six years for men and 10 years for women." Yet 41% of seniors do not feel that the transportation support in their community is adequate, says the NCOA.

Having access to adequate public transportation or other senior transportation services is key to seniors' accessing programs and resources, as well as their feelings of connectedness and independence.

14. Caregivers of the elderly are also at risk for social isolation.

Being a family caregiver is an enormous responsibility, whether you are caring for a parent, spouse, or other relative. When that person has Alzheimer's disease, dementia, or a physical impairment, the caregiver may feel even less able to set aside his or her caregiving duties to attend to social relationships they previously enjoyed. This can trigger loneliness and depression. Seeking support, caring for yourself, and even looking for temporary respite care can help ward off caregiver loneliness and restore your sense of connection.

15. Loneliness can be contagious.

Studies have found that loneliness has a tendency to spread from person to person, due to negative social interactions and other factors. In other words, when one person is lonely, that loneliness is more likely to spread to friends or contacts of the lonely individual. Making things even worse, people have a tendency to further isolate people who are lonely because we have evolved to avoid threats to our social cohesion.

It's a complicated situation, and simply telling seniors to engage in more social activities may not be enough. Considering our loved ones' needs as individuals is a valuable first step to figuring out how to prevent or combat isolation.

16. Lonely people are more likely to engage in unhealthy behavior.

A 2011 study using data from the English Longitudinal Study of Aging found that people who are socially isolated or lonely are also more likely to report risky health behaviors such as poor diet, lack of physical activity, and smoking. Conversely, social support can help encourage seniors to eat well, exercise, and live healthy lifestyles.

Living in a community situation can be an effective barrier to loneliness, and most senior communities specifically promote wellness through diet and exercise programs.

17. Volunteering can reduce social isolation and loneliness in seniors.

We all know that volunteering is a rewarding activity, and seniors have a unique skill set and oodles of life experience to contribute to their communities. It can also boost longevity and contribute to mental health and well-being, and it ensures that seniors have a source of social connection. There are plenty of opportunities tailor-made for seniors interested in volunteering, which can be found on websites such as allforgood.org, foodforward.org, retiredbrains.com, seniorcorps.org, voa.org (Volunteers of America), nationalservice.gov, and volunteermatch.org.

18. Feeling isolated? Take a class.

A review of studies looking at various types of interventions on senior loneliness found that the most effective programs for combating isolation had an educational or training component: for instance, classes on health-related topics, computer training, or exercise classes.

19. Technology can help senior isolation—but not always.

Even though modern technology provides us with more opportunities than ever for keeping in touch, sometimes the result is that we feel lonelier than ever. The key to finding technological interventions that really do help is matching those interventions to the specific needs of individual seniors.

One simple strategy that does help: for seniors with hearing loss, simply providing a hearing aid can improve communication and reduce loneliness. Phone contact and Internet-based support programs were less consistent in their effectiveness, but for some, they might provide a lifeline.

20. Physical activity reduces senior isolation.

Group exercise programs, it turns out, are a wonderfully effective way to reduce isolation and loneliness in seniors—and of course they have the added benefit of being great for physical and mental health. In one study, seniors reported greater well-being regardless of whether the activity was aerobic or lower-impact, like stretching.

Senior isolation is neither inevitable nor irreversible. Getting the facts can help us prevent loneliness in our senior loved ones as they face the life changes of aging.

Chapter 2

Isolation: The Cruelest Form of Elder Abuse

by Linda Kincaid

Linda Kincaid was a public health professional and safety consultant to high-tech companies for two decades before her mother was kidnapped, held prisoner, and isolated in an assisted living facility. Linda was fortunate in retaining a trial attorney who obtained a temporary restraining order against isolation elder abuse. The restraining order secured the abused elder's right to visitation. Family was allowed to visit within hours of the court hearing. Following the ordeal, Linda brought her training in root cause analysis to the issue of elder abuse and elder rights. Responding to law enforcement apathy and systemic failure that are so prevalent in elder abuse cases, Linda cofounded Coalition for Elder & Disability Rights (CEDAR). Isolation elder abuse of Carol Hahn (Linda's mother) was the impetus for the nation's first legislation on right to visitation. Certain names have been changed for reasons of privacy.

California enacted the nation's first legislation clarifying an elder's right to visitation with loved ones. Our legislature passed Assembly Bill 937 (2013) in response to extended and unlawful isolation of my mother, Carol Hahn. Governor Jerry Brown signed AB 937 into law on September 19, 2013, two days after Mom died. Our family honors my mother's memory by advocating for other vulnerable individuals to enjoy the rights and freedoms that my mother was denied.

All elder abuse is harmful. Abuse crushes the spirit and destroys the dignity of the elder. Isolation abuse is particularly insidious. Hidden from the watchful eyes of family and friends, isolated elders fall victim to increasingly horrific forms of abuse. Emotional abuse, physical abuse, sexual abuse, and chemical restraint all occur in long-term care facilities. Subpoenaed documents in my mother's case contain many indicators of sexual assaults by a male caregiver who worked alone on

California Advocates for Nursing Home Reform (CANHR) is considered one of the nation's leading advocacy groups for elder rights. *CANHR's Visitation Guide for California Long Term Care Facilities and Hospitals* contains guidance and relevant statutes for California and the nation:

"The right to visit with people is among our most sacred personal rights. Even the US Constitution guarantees a right to visit by preventing federal or state governments from abridging our freedom to associate. . . .

"California Assembly Bill 937 (Wieckowski, 2013) amended Cal. Probate Code 2531, clarifying once and for all that conservators, California's strongest form of surrogate, may not control a conservatee's visitation or other personal rights unless a specific court order is made. If conservators need special court orders, weaker forms of surrogate like agents or family members need special court orders."

the night shift. Medication records show escalating chemical restraint to silence my mother's cries for help. California Advocates for Nursing Home Reform (CANHR) comments:

> Visitation is extremely important to hospital patients and residents of long- term care facilities. Studies show that visitation is highly correlated with improved quality of life for patients and residents.

Imprisonment and Isolation in Assisted Living Facility

My mother began showing signs of dementia in 2006. As her memories faded, we were committed to finding the best care possible. But family had no role in Mom's care after she was taken from her home.

By June 2010, my mother's memories were clouded by Alzheimer's disease. Mom's step-granddaughter "Jennifer" seized control of my mother and her estate. Within days, Jennifer had control of the assets. She engaged an attorney to execute a power of attorney for finances and a power of attorney for health care, both naming Jennifer as agent for my mother. Jennifer engaged the attorney to execute a trust with Jennifer as trustee for my mother. The attorney later testified that Jennifer did not share any information about my mother's cognitive decline of the previous years. He testified that he believed I was estranged from my mother and had no contact with her since I was eight years old.

Having seized control of my mother's assets, Jennifer hid my mother in an assisted living facility in Yucaipa, CA. Facility records show that Mom slept on a mattress on the floor. Caregiver logs indicate that Mom sometimes received no fluids for over twenty-four hours. At times, she passed no urine for over eight hours. Jennifer placed my mother on hospice and discontinued routine medical care, including treatment for my mother's very painful rheumatoid arthritis. Hospice records establish that Mom was unable to hold a fork and could not feed herself. But facility care plans instructed staff to feed Mom only a few bites of each meal, and then hand her the fork. Hospice records repeatedly confirmed the muscle wasting and severe cachexia that occur with starvation.

Jennifer and her attorneys incorrectly asserted that her power of attorney for health care gave her absolute authority over my mother and all aspects of her care. Paid by my mother's estate, Jennifer's attorneys opposed my mother moving from the abusive facility, and they opposed my mother receiving needed medical care. Social services agencies, law enforcement, and the court failed to intervene.

Probate Code 4689
"Nothing in this division authorizes an agent under a power of attorney for health care to make a health care decision if the principal objects to the decision. If the principal objects to the health care decision of the agent under a power of attorney, the matter shall be governed by the law that would apply if there were no power of attorney for health care."

On July 2, 2010, Jennifer had not yet taken my mother's cell phone. Mom called me for help. Mom did not know where she was or how she got there, but she was certain that she wanted family to help her escape. Jennifer instructed facility staff not to allow me on the property. Jennifer later testified that she kept me away from Mom to prevent me from becoming power of attorney or recovering my mother's assets.

On July 3, 2010, I called the facility where Jennifer hid my mother. The executive director said that she would not allow me to see my mother unless I brought a letter from an attorney. The executive director later testified that she was following instructions from her vice president of operations.

On July 4, 2010, an attorney drafted a letter establishing my mother's cognitive impairments. Our attorney's letter urged the facility to recognize me as my mother's next of kin and her rightful agent for health care decisions.

On July 5, 2010, we arrived at the facility and called San Bernardino County Sheriff's Department for a "civil standby" so a deputy would escort us into the facility. We entered the facility and presented the letter from our attorney. The assistant director refused to accept the letter, but she allowed a brief visit with my mother. Forgetting that I was her only child, Mom asked about her other daughters. Mom confused me with Jennifer asking, "How is the other Linda? The Linda in San Diego?"

Then my mother became distraught about not having any money. I attempted to calm her by explaining that Jennifer put her money into a joint account and was paying her bills for her. Mom exclaimed, "That's wrong. Jennifer shouldn't have done that."

The assistant director immediately ordered us off the property. As she escorted me to the door she stated, "You won't be allowed to see your mother again." A few minutes later, the executive director repeated those words. "You won't be allowed to see your mother again." The deputy was present throughout the brief visit and did nothing to secure my mother's rights.

On July 8, 2010, Mom and I had the last phone call we were allowed for several months. Mom was distraught and frightened for her life. She said she found copies of Jennifer's estate planning documents in her room. Mom had no memory of signing the documents, and she was terrified of what they could mean. I tried to calm my mother. A

California Civil Codes on Elder Abuse

Welfare and Institutions Code 15610.07(a)
"Abuse of an elder or a dependent adult means any of the following:
(1) Physical abuse, neglect, abandonment, isolation, abduction, or other treatment with resulting physical harm or pain or mental suffering.
(2) The deprivation by a care custodian of goods or services that are necessary to avoid physical harm or mental suffering.
(3) Financial abuse, as defined in Section 15610.30."

Welfare and Institutions Code 15610.43(a)
"'Isolation' means any of the following:
(1) Acts intentionally committed for the purpose of preventing, and that do serve to prevent, an elder or dependent adult from receiving his or her mail or telephone calls.
(2) Telling a caller or prospective visitor that an elder or dependent adult is not present, or does not wish to talk with the caller, or does not wish to meet with the visitor where the statement is false, is contrary to the express wishes of the elder or the dependent adult, whether he or she is competent or not, and is made for the purpose of preventing the elder or dependent adult from having contact with family, friends, or concerned persons.
(3) False imprisonment, as defined in Section 236 of the Penal Code.

> (4) Physical restraint of an elder or dependent adult, for
>   the purpose of preventing the elder or dependent
>   adult from meeting with visitors."
>
> *Penal Code 236.*
> False imprisonment is the unlawful violation of the personal
> liberty of another.

friend called our local Santa Clara County Sheriff's Department for an officer to come take a telephone statement from my mother. Two deputies arrived quickly, but they refused to take a statement. They left without preparing a report.

A San Bernardino County sheriff's deputy responded to my mother's location and took her cell phone from her. The deputy ordered me not to call my mother again. He threatened to arrest me if I tried to visit my mother. He threatened to charge me with a crime if I reported his misconduct. The deputy later testified, "I was chewing her out pretty good."

On July 9, 2010, the assistant director of the facility told me, "Carol Hahn is allowed no visitors and no phone calls. All calls go through Jennifer." My mother cut off from all contact with her loved ones.

On July 17, 2010, the duty sergeant for the Yucaipa substation sent an email stating, "The [assisted living facility] has instructed their staff to call the police and report any further actions by Linda Kincaid and her associates as criminal acts. Linda Kincaid and her associates are considered trespassing if they are located anywhere on the property of the facility. Any further telephone calls may be considered as annoying and threatening."

Violation of Right to Phone Calls

Each time a family member tried to call my mother on the facility phone, the call was denied. Our attorney Steven Haney asked the executive director, "And was it your understanding that Jennifer had the right to limit or deprive Carol Hahn of her personal rights to receive phone calls from whoever she wanted?" The executive director testified, "To my understanding, because of the power of attorney, that is what we did. We followed what she said." Haney dug deeper: "And if the resident and the person holding the power of attorney, have a difference

Excerpts from *Personal Rights, Residential Care Facilities for the Elderly (California)*

"(6) To leave or depart the facility at any time and to not be locked into any room, building, or on facility premises by day or night. This does not prohibit the establishment of house rules, such as the locking of doors at night, for the protection of residents; nor does it prohibit, with permission of the licensing agency, the barring of windows against intruders.

"(9) To have communications to the facility from his/her family and responsible persons answered promptly and appropriately.

"(11) To have his/her visitors, including ombudspersons and advocacy representatives permitted to visit privately during reasonable hours and without prior notice, provided that the rights of other residents are not infringed upon.

"(14) To have reasonable access to telephones, to both make and receive confidential calls. The licensee may require reimbursement for long distance calls."

of opinion, you follow what the person holding the power of attorney says with respect to allowance of phone calls from family members?" The executive director testified, "To my understanding, we follow the power of attorney."

Violation of Right to Visitation

On September 27, 2010, Community Care Licensing (CCL), the state agency that licenses and oversees assisted living facilities in California, cited the facility for violating my mother's right to visitation, as stated in Welfare and Institutions Code 87468(a)(11). The assistant director signed the citation, but she continued to deny visitation.

On October 4, 2010, the facility appealed the citation. The executive director wrote, "First, the resident has a notarized Power of Attorney which is acting in the best interest of her charge. They have asked that the particular visitor not be allowed to see this resident because at the time of the visit the resident became upset when they said they were going to moving [sic] her."

On October 18, 2010, the facility Tenant Service Notes instructed staff, "Resident is to NOT have any visitors other than [Jennifer]."

On January 20, 2011, CCL denied the appeal. Their denial letter stated, "The decision to allow or disallow any visitation belongs to the resident alone unless the courts have appointed a conservator over the person and granted the conservator the power to make such decisions. A notarized power of attorney is insufficient to divest this right." The Executive Director disregarded the denial letter.

My mother was isolated from June 2010 until September 2011, shortly after we retained Los Angeles litigation attorney Steven Haney. Haney petitioned the court for a Temporary Restraining Order against isolation abuse. We visited my mother that same day. The effort to secure my mother's right to visitation required sixteen court hearings and cost family $70,000 in legal fees. The cost to my mother was far greater. During the time she was isolated, my mother became incontinent, she lost the ability to walk, and she lost memories of her closest family members.

> **California Advocates for Nursing Home Reform (CANHR) provides guidance on residents' right to visitation:**
>
> "A residential care facility for the elderly ("RCFE") is a type of living arrangement for people 60 years of age or over who need some help with daily living. . . . As in nursing homes, residents of RCFEs (commonly known as 'assisted living facilities') have the right to visit privately with anyone of their choosing in the facility, including family, friends, Ombudsman, and advocates, for meetings without prior notice. . . . RCFE residents are not limited to having visitors in the facility. They can see their friends and family off-site because they have the right to leave the facility at any time. Residents cannot be locked into any room, building, or in any part of the facility unless they or a court-appointed conservator have consented."

Social Services Agencies

During the fifteen months the facility isolated my mother, we researched every available resource concerning elder abuse. California's Department of Justice (DOJ) instructs victims and their families to report elder abuse to Adult Protective Services (APS), the long-term care ombudsman, and CCL. Each of those agencies substantiated that the facility isolated my mother. But social service agencies have no authority to intervene in elder abuse.

In July 2010, an APS investigator substantiated that the facility isolated my mother from family. The investigator later testified that she referred the case to the San Bernardino County Sheriff's Department. APS staff are social workers, not law enforcement. Enforcing elder abuse law falls to police, not APS.

Adult Protective Services (APS)

"Each California County has an Adult Protective Services (APS) agency to help elder adults (65 years and older) and dependent adults (18–64 who are disabled), when these adults are unable to meet their own needs, or are victims of abuse, neglect or exploitation. County APS agencies investigate reports of abuse of elders and dependent adults who live in private homes, apartments, hotels or hospitals.

"APS staff also provides information and referral to other agencies and educates the public about reporting requirements and responsibilities under the Elder and Dependent Adult Abuse Reporting laws."

Source: http://www.cdss.ca.gov/agedblinddisabled/PG1298.htm

In July 2010, a long-term care ombudsman told me, "What calls your mother is allowed to receive are being overseen by a deputy out of the Yucaipa substation." She later testified that she notified the facility in July 2010 and again in August 2010 that residents have the right to visitors. There was nothing more she could do. Like APS workers, ombudsmen are social workers with no enforcement authority.

Ombudsmen are further hampered by confidentiality regulations. If a resident lacks capacity to give informed consent, then the ombudsman is prohibited from reporting abuse to law enforcement. My mother lacked capacity to give consent. Naturally, Jennifer did not give consent. The ombudsman later testified that County Counsel instructed her not to investigate our continued complaints of isolation.

Long-Term Care Ombudsman Program

"The goal of the State Long-Term Care Ombudsman Program is to advocate for the rights of all residents of long-term care facilities. The Ombudsman's advocacy role takes two forms: 1) to receive and resolve individual complaints and issues by, or on behalf of, these residents; and 2) to pursue resident advocacy in the long-term care system, its laws, policies, regulations, and administration through public education and consensus building. Residents or their family members can file a complaint directly with the local Long-Term Care Ombudsman or by calling the CRISISline. All long-term care facilities are required to post, in a conspicuous location, the phone number for the local Ombudsman office and the Statewide CRISISline number 1-800-231-4024. This CRISISline is available 24 hours a day, 7 days a week to take calls and refer complaints from residents."

Source: http://www.aging.ca.gov/programs/ltcop/

Throughout 2010 and 2011, we submitted many complaints to CCL. Our phone calls were not returned. Subpoenaed records show that CCL management in Sacramento knew the local office disregarded our complaints. CCL never reported the abuse to law enforcement, as California law requires them to do.

Community Care Licensing

"The Community Care Licensing Division's (CCLD) mission is to promote the health, safety, and quality of life of each person in community care through the administration of an effective collaborative regulatory enforcement system. This is accomplished by:
- Promoting strategies to increase voluntary compliance
- Providing technical assistance to and consulting with care providers
- Working collaboratively with clients, their families, advocates, care providers, placement agencies, related programs and regulatory agencies, and others involved in community care
- Training staff in all aspects of the licensing process
- Educating the public about CCLD and community care options
- Promoting continuous improvement and efficiency throughout the community care licensing system"

Source: http://www.cdss.ca.gov/inforesources/Senior-Care-Licensing

Isolation Abuse May Be Common in Long-term Care Facilities

In the summer of 2010, we interviewed twenty-five assisted living facilities in central San Bernardino County. Twenty-four of the twenty-five facilities said they would isolate a resident if the person paying the bill made that request. The director of one facility incorrectly stated that individuals give up all personal rights when they sign a power of attorney.

California Penal Code Section 368.5

"(a) Local law enforcement agencies and state law enforcement agencies with jurisdiction shall have concurrent jurisdiction to investigate elder and dependent adult abuse and all other crimes against elder victims and victims with disabilities.

(b) Adult protective services agencies and local long-term care ombudsman programs also have jurisdiction within their statutory authority to investigate elder and dependent adult abuse and criminal neglect, and may assist local law enforcement agencies in criminal investigations at the law enforcement agencies' request, provided, however, that law enforcement agencies shall retain exclusive responsibility for criminal investigations, any provision of law to the contrary notwithstanding."

As elder rights advocates, we receive many calls from distraught families trying to contact isolated loved ones. Law enforcement rarely intervenes in isolation elder abuse. Injunctive relief through civil court is very slow, very expensive, and very unreliable. Media attention and public pressure are the only tactics that we have found to be consistently effective in securing the rights of elder abuse victims.

Chapter 3

Financial Exploitation

Elder financial exploitation has been called the crime of the twenty-first century, and deploying effective interventions has never been more important. Older people are attractive targets because they often have assets and regular income. These consumers may be especially vulnerable due to isolation, cognitive decline, physical disability, health problems, or bereavemeant. Elder financial exploitation robs victims of their resources, dignity, and quality of life—and those victims may never recover from it. Financial institutions play a vital role in prevention in responding to this type of elder abuse. Banks and credit unions are uniquely positioned to detect that an elder account holder has been targeted and to take action.

Quite simply, banks must develop, implement, and maintain internal protocols and procedures to protect account holders from elder financial exploitation.

A variety of behaviors and account activities may signal that a consumer is the victim of elder financial exploitation. These warning signs are not proof of financial exploitation; rather, they are signs that should trigger investigation and other proactive measures. Due to the revolving nature of fraud in the methods by which exploitation is perpetrated, the Consumer Financial Protection Bureau (CFPB) encourages financial institutions to maintain an up-to-date list of behaviors and activities that indicate fraud risk of older consumers. The CFPB compiled the following list of risk indicators from several sources.

Warning Signs of Elder Financial Abuse

Interactions with older consumers, caregivers, and other third parties

1. A previously uninvolved relative, caregiver, or friend begins conducting financial transactions on behalf of an older consumer—or claims access or privileges to the consumer's private information—without proper documentation.

2. An older consumer associates with new "friends" or strangers.

3. A caregiver or other third party shows excessive interest in the older consumer's finances or accounts, does not allow the consumer to speak for him or herself, or is reluctant to leave the older consumer's side during interactions with the financial institution.

4. An older consumer exhibits an unusual degree of fear, anxiety, submissiveness, or deference to a caregiver or other third party.

5. An older person expresses excitement over financial opportunity, price, or windfall.

6. An elder consumer lacks knowledge about his or her personal financial status or accounts, or is reluctant to discuss financial matters.

7. An older consumer appears to neglect or experience a decline in appearance, grooming, or hygiene.

Unusual Account Activity

1. Large increases in account activity, such as daily maximum withdrawals from an ATM.

2. Large gaps in check numbers or out-of-sync check numbers.

3. Uncharacteristic non-sufficient funds activity or overdrafts.

4. Uncharacteristic debit transactions (including unusual ATM use).

5. Uncharacteristic lapses in payments for services.

6. Disregard for penalties when closing accounts or certificates of deposit.

7. Abrupt changes to financial documents, such as a new power of attorney, a change to a joint account, or a change in account beneficiary.

8. Excessive numbers of payments or payments of large sums to a caregiver or third party.

9. New account created soon after you add an authorized user.

10. Statements mailed to an address separate from customer's residence.

11. No activity on an active account or joint account.

12. Signatures that do not match or appear suspicious.

13. Uncharacteristic requests to wire money.

Key recommendations:

You should only use banks that properly train management and staff to prevent, detect, and respond to suspected elder abuse, who train personnel regularly and frequently and tailor training to specific staff roles. Training should cover warning signs that may signal financial exploitation, including behavior and transactions that are red flags, and take action steps to prevent exploitation and respond to suspicious events. The best banks use technology to monitor for signs of elder financial exploitation. Because indicators of elder fraud risk may differ from conventional accepted patterns of suspicious activity, financial institutions using predictive analytics will review their filtering criteria against individual account holders' patterns and explore additional risk factors that may be associated with elder financial exploitation.

Why Elder Financial Exploitation is so Challenging

The following is taken from written testimony to the United States Senate Special Committee on Aging by **Page Ulrey***, senior deputy prosecuting attorney for the King County Prosecutor's Office in Seattle, Washington, who has been her office's dedicated elder abuse prosecutor, handling cases of elder financial exploitation, neglect, physical assault, sexual assault, and homicide for 15 years.*

In case after case of elder financial exploitation that I have handled, I have witnessed the huge human and economic toll the problem takes. Its victims suffer tremendously from the betrayal and the loss of their life savings, often dying premature deaths as a result of it. Families are torn apart by it, with the damage often lasting for generations. And federal and state governments often end up bearing the cost of the exploitation, due to the depletion of the elder's assets, the increase in their care needs, and the increased demand on Medicare, Medicaid, and other health, housing, and social programs.

This testimony addresses: 1) why elder financial exploitation cases are so challenging for the criminal justice system; and 2) offers recommendations for action that can be taken by Congress and federal agencies to begin to address the problem more effectively.

Why Elder Financial Exploitation Poses a Problem for the Criminal Justice System

Having historically deemed most cases of elder abuse as "civil" or "family" matters, the criminal justice system is only now beginning to come to terms with the fact that crimes are being inflicted on the elderly at alarming rates, and that only a small fraction of those crimes are ever properly investigated and prosecuted. As a result, we are woefully ill equipped to handle these cases, both in terms of knowledge and resources. Compounding the problem is the fact that elder financial exploitation often involves co-occurring crime types, including neglect and physical and sexual assault; rarely are there prosecutors, law enforcement, victim service providers, or other responders who have expertise in all types. In my experience, financial exploitation is one of the crime types with which the justice system struggles the most.

Elder financial exploitation cases are far more complex than typical theft cases, as they often involve powers of attorney, guardianships, fiduciary duties, trusts, wills, mortgages, and issues of capacity and undue influence. Knowledge of these concepts is essential to properly investigating and prosecuting cases with financial dimensions, yet few in the criminal justice system are familiar with them all. Rarely, if ever, are these subjects taught in police academies or in training for 911 dispatchers.

While they may be taught in law school, they are seldom included in the curriculum of criminal law or prosecutor training courses.

Because victims of elder financial exploitation are so often isolated, their victimization often goes on for months and sometimes years before it is discovered. When it is discovered, the lack of training on these concepts at every level of the criminal justice system means that the likelihood of a door being closed in the face of the person reporting the wrongdoing is high. From the 911 dispatcher to the patrol officer to the detective to the prosecutor—if just one of these essential players fails to recognize a report as criminal, the case will likely end there, with the exploitation continuing until Adult Protective Services (APS) or the family intervenes civilly, or no one at all intervenes. In any event, the elder's resources are usually gone. Even if there are assets left when the case reaches someone in the justice system who recognizes it as potentially criminal, rarely does that person have the knowledge or legal tools to seize the funds so that they can be returned to the victim.

In the rare case when a report of elder financial exploitation does make it through the door and onto the desk of a detective or prosecutor, other hurdles exist. In the majority of cases that my elder abuse unit sees, the victim has some degree of cognitive impairment. The defense raised most often is that the victim "consented" to giving the perpetrator his/her assets. In order to refute this claim of consent, we must obtain an evaluation of the victim by a geriatrician or neuropsychologist or psychiatrist with expertise in dementia. Most police agencies and prosecutors' offices have no connections to such experts and lack the funding to pay for such an evaluation. Adult Protective Services may have access to experts who can assist in such an evaluation; however, APS often lacks the tools, resources, and training to screen for cognitive impairment itself when there are concerns that it might be present. As a result, APS often unwittingly screens out cases involving victims who lack the cognitive capacity to handle complex financial transactions, thereby allowing the exploitation to continue.

Additionally, in most of these cases, the complete financial records of the victim and suspect are essential parts of the evidence. Once these records are obtained, they must be entered into spreadsheets and analyzed. Most detectives do not have access to a forensic accountant and so are left to attempt to conduct this analysis on their own—an often daunting and unappealing task for a criminal investigator, particularly if he or she hasn't been trained in how to investigate financial crimes. In my office, the King County Prosecuting Attorney's office, we saw a significant change in our ability to pursue elder abuse cases with a financial component after we hired a forensic accountant to help us with the financial aspects of the investigation. Our forensic accountant knows what records we need, how to analyze them, and is able to convey what those records show in a way juries can understand.

Further complicating financial exploitation cases is the fact that they so often occur in the same case with neglect, physical abuse, and even sexual abuse. When we see a neglect or abuse case, often the investigation turns up financial exploitation. The reverse is also true: where there is financial exploitation, we often see abuse or neglect. And usually, the different types of mistreatment are linked.

In a typical neglect scenario, for example, the elder is cared for in their own home by an adult family member and dies of sepsis (blood infection) due to multiple, large, untreated, or improperly treated pressure ulcers (bedsores). If the case is to be handled properly, both its medical and financial aspects must be investigated. The financial aspects of the case should be looked into to determine whether the neglect was financially motivated and thus potentially criminal, or caused by self-neglect or the caregiver's lack of knowledge, in which case it is not. What we often find in these cases is significant financial exploitation, with the caregiver motivated to not provide necessary treatment in hopes of a larger inheritance, to hasten the elder's death, or to avoid paying for proper care so they can continue spending the elder's assets. The medical aspects of the case must be investigated in order to determine whether the pressure sores were caused by neglect versus underlying disease process. However, as in financial cases, most police agencies and prosecutor's offices do not have relationships with the appropriate medical experts who can assist them. In our jurisdiction, we are lucky to have a chief medical examiner, Dr. Richard Harruff, who is a leading expert in neglect cases and knows to refer the matter and what kinds of questions to ask. Most medical examiners and coroners, however, lack knowledge and expertise on the subject of adult neglect and when it might be criminal, let alone its nexus to financial motivations. Even if they are trained, many are loath to conduct autopsies and make findings on cases of neglect, fearing that their already overburdened agencies will be unable to handle the onslaught of new cases that will ensue as a result.

Besides being underreported by the public, elder financial exploitation is also underreported by all sorts of professionals who may have reason to suspect something is amiss, including health professionals, social service professionals, long-term care professionals, and others, many of whom are required by law to report their suspicions. In my state, as in others, the law requires that any mandatory reporters [those required by statute to report criminal activity] report financial exploitation cases only to Adult Protective Services, not to law enforcement. However, in addition to lacking the proper tools and resources to screen for capacity impairment, APS also often lacks the tools, resources, and expertise to properly investigate these cases. As a result, many of the cases of financial exploitation that are reported to APS are never referred on to law enforcement.

Adding to these difficulties are the often pressing needs of the victim, who may be suffering from dementia, health issues, physical disabilities, financial and legal issues, isolation, fear of loss of independence, need for housing, and lack of caregiver and social support and advocacy. While APS may be able to assist by locating services for the victim, APS does not provide those services, and is not an advocate for the victim. Because there is no advocacy available for victims of elder financial crimes in most communities, it is not at all unusual for the detective or prosecutor to be drawn into playing that role, if any-one takes it on. Additionally, due to the current lack of coordination between the criminal justice system and civil legal services on these cases, many victims are never referred to civil attorneys to assist them in recouping losses and repairing their credit and the other damage that has been done as a result of the exploitation.

In addition, the relatively robust victim assistance network that exists for other victims of crime often does not extend to older crime victims who usually have distinct needs and desires not met by existing services.

When the victim of elder financial exploitation is unlucky enough to be scammed by someone from another country, the chances of crim-inal justice involvement are even lower, due to lack of resources and coordination between local law enforcement and the federal agencies that are beginning to investigate and respond to these cases.

Yet another aspect of the problem is that the parties responsible for elder financial exploitation may be long-term care facilities or other pro-viders of health care or other services that take an older person's money but don't provide the care or services promised or that the elder needs. When a victim is in a long-term care or other facility, law enforcement experiences yet another set of problems: unfamiliarity with the facility's organizational structure; difficulty obtaining records; state investiga-tion and licensing agencies that are often reluctant to report or coop-erate; and systemic failures that make finding and charging individual suspects challenging if not impossible.

What Can Be Done: Three First Steps

My recommendation of three important first steps that should be taken is as follows:

1. Develop infrastructure to support criminal justice handling of elder abuse cases at the local, state, and federal level.

With the passage of the Child Abuse Prevention and Treatment Act (CAPTA) in 1974 and the Violence Against Women Act (VAWA) in 1994, the federal government made tremendous strides in building the infrastructure to respond to child abuse, domestic violence, and sexual assault, not only at the federal and state level, but also at the local level. There is a profound need for similar attention by the federal government to the issue of elder abuse.

One common ingredient that I have seen in communities whose criminal justice systems are beginning to respond properly to elder abuse is [the use of] specialized prosecutors, detectives, and victim advocates, as we see in child abuse, domestic violence, and sexual assault cases. When these professionals have been trained on the complex concepts involved in these cases, and when they are not simultaneously faced with competing cases, elder abuse reports are investigated, charges are filed, and victims' needs are addressed. Further, these professionals are much more likely to be active and committed participants in their community's various elder abuse Multi-Disciplinary Teams (MDTs). In addition, medical and social service providers, APS, financial services professionals, and the public have an identified person to call when they come across an elder abuse case that is serious enough that it may warrant suspicion and perhaps a criminal response. Once the community begins to believe that the justice system will actually take action on these cases, then reporting, documentation, coordination, and investigations across disciplines will improve. Creation of elder abuse specialist positions in the justice system is necessary not only at the local level, but at the state and federal level as well, so that the many cases that occur across state and national borders and in long-term care and other facilities receiving federal funding are also responded to properly.

But creation of these positions alone isn't sufficient. In order for professionals placed in them to succeed, they need technical assistance, information, resources, enhanced knowledge, and ongoing training. Some of these resources exist at the federal level, in various states, and in some organizations, but few local police, prosecutors, or victim services providers are aware of them. We need to fund a systematic federal effort to reach out to these professionals at the state and local level, connect them to the resources that already exist, and continue to develop resources for them.

We also need a National Resource Center for the Investigation and Prosecution of Elder Abuse with experienced prosecutors and detectives on staff to provide advice, case consultation, and technical assistance, and to incorporate the elder abuse website that Department of Justice (DOJ) is currently developing. Further, we need to fund the creation of multidisciplinary forensic centers within states so that victims will benefit from a more coordinated response from APS, law enforcement (federal, state and local), medical professionals, forensic professionals, financial services institutions, aging network entities, the long-term care ombudsman, and others.

2. Develop and conduct training.

As I have described above, there is a pressing need for training of the law enforcement officers and detectives, prosecutors, judges, Adult Protective Services workers, financial services professionals, and others who see and routinely respond to these cases. I am a member of the national training team for the Enhanced Training and Services to End Abuse in Later Life Program, a small grant project of the Office on Violence Against Women. This project is doing just that: funding communities to conduct systematic training of these professionals on how to recognize and properly respond to all forms of elder abuse. In the years that I have been working on this project, I have watched as transformations have taken place in many of the communities that have been awarded the grant, including my own. However, OVW only has the funding to train a handful of communities each year, so it is very slow going.

In addition to training those whose job it is to respond to these cases, we need to train the professionals across all disciplines in positions to reduce the problem, and we need both discipline-specific and multidisciplinary trainings to do so. This was also a priority identified in the Elder Justice Roadmap Project. The National Center on Elder Abuse has a webpage with links to existing curricula, training videos, events, and other resources. In addition, efforts are underway to inventory existing training and education resources and identify what is still needed. One such gap was recently filled by the Department of Justice-funded Online Elder Abuse Training for Legal Services Providers—a much-needed resource for civil attorneys to hone their skills to prevent and assist victims of financial exploitation and other forms of elder abuse. We need to continue to develop, coordinate, implement, and update these trainings so that we are routinely conducting them for professionals such as accountants, bank employees, financial advisors, investment professionals, and others in the financial services industry, as well as paramedics and emergency medical personnel, ombudsmen, physicians, nurses, forensic experts, social workers, notaries public, and private civil attorneys, to name a few.

3. Increase knowledge.

In order to begin to respond properly to these cases, there are many areas in which research and data collection are desperately needed. We need to fund, pilot test, and collect data on the impact of specialized elder abuse detectives, prosecutors, and victim advocates in a few jurisdictions. Additionally, we should expand a small exploratory project funded by DOJ's Bureau of Justice Statistics in the King County Prosecutor's Office to track and evaluate what types of elder abuse cases law enforcement and prosecutors are seeing, which ones they pursue and why, [and] where cases originate. [We should further check] what types of referrals, reporting, and investigations make for successful prosecutions, the impact of prosecution on victims, and how the prosecution response is affected by issues such as capacity, lack of a living victim, victims who cannot or choose not to cooperate, lack of prosecutors and/or detectives who specialize in elder abuse cases, the impact of the presence or absence of APS involvement, MDT involvement, use of experts, and the availability of victim advocacy. Developing this information about the impact of the justice system's involvement and other factors will help us to target scarce resources where they can be put to the best use.

We also urgently need research about forensic markers—specifically on how to tell when neglect caused and led to the worsening of pressure ulcers, on fractures, dehydration, and malnutrition, and on other physical signs and symptoms with a nexus to elder abuse. We need to know more about the connection between the refusal of care/intervention and dementia, as it is very often a hindrance to APS and law enforcement intervention and to successful prosecution.

We also need to know more about the prevalence of elder abuse so that law enforcement and prosecution offices can better understand the nature and extent of the problem. In addition, we need more research on and better tools for the detection and assessment of cognitive (in)capacity, especially as it relates to the vulnerability to elder financial exploitation and abuse, and the ability to "consent" to being exploited, neglected, or abused. Finally, we need to assess and pilot test tools for financial services professionals that enable them to better identify, report, and address situations involving elder financial exploitation.

Other Recommendations

The needs of the criminal justice system extend well beyond the first steps I have articulated above. Below is a list of other recommendations that would, over the long term, make a tremendous difference in how we respond to these cases:

- Enhanced victim services (in justice system offices and the community) to assist victims, provide advocacy, and connect them with services and civil legal assistance;
- Improved reporting and referral systems so that suspected or confirmed elder abuse cases are directed to the right entity to protect victims, stop wrongdoing, prevent future victimization, recompense losses, and, if appropriate, prosecute wrongdoers. Entities including law enforcement, prosecution, APS, state agencies that license long-term care facilities, social services, financial services, and health care providers should become more aware of criteria for prioritization of response, standardized referral methods, and how to determine which cases should be referred to which agency;
- Strengthening of the civil legal role in preventing elder abuse and responding to cases of elder abuse, including assisting victims with protection orders, powers of attorney and guardianships, recovering stolen assets, and restoring credit after financial exploitation has occurred, regardless of whether the case is appropriate for criminal action;
- Development and funding of forfeiture units or positions within prosecutors' offices so that the stolen assets and funds of older victims can be frozen and recovered without the expense and hardship of a civil lawsuit;
- Legislation and guidelines to assist state and local prosecutors in obtaining copies of federal tax returns, to improve their

ability to build a financial exploitation case, especially in cases where the perpetrator invokes the "gift" defense;

- Funding and support for the creation of investigative/law enforcement positions at the federal level that are focused on cons and scams of older victims so that federal, state, and local prosecutors are better equipped to address this billion-dollar industry;

- Legislation and training to improve reporting of elder abuse by financial institutions when they have reason to believe their client is the victim of a financial crime. This can be particularly complicated when the apparent perpetrator has power of attorney or is a guardian;

- Legislation and standards to monitor proxy decision-makers (such as powers of attorney, guardians, and representative payees) who have huge power over older persons' assets and few checks to assure compliance with their legal fiduciary duties;

- Legislation and training to improve recognition and reporting by health care providers of all forms of elder abuse;

- Improved training and funding for medical examiners and coroners to improve their recognition and assumption of jurisdiction of potential elder neglect deaths;

- Funding for data collection for medical examiners and coroners for the review of elder deaths and participation in Elder Fatality Review Teams;

- Legislation and regulations to improve reporting by state agencies who license and investigate abuse and neglect in long-term care facilities to law enforcement;

- Data collection on the impact of mandatory reporting on elder abuse victim safety, improving civil attorneys' ability to report suspected elder abuse without fear of liability, and giving them the tools they need to prevent their older clients from becoming victimized in the first place.

Conclusion

As I hope is obvious from this chapter, our need for an improved response to elder financial exploitation (and the abuse and neglect that so often accompany it) is immense and urgent. Implementing solutions at modest cost is within reach and a great investment with the potential to save untold suffering and billions of dollars. We don't have to reinvent the wheel to do this. Already throughout the country, government and non-governmental agencies and individuals are working hard on many aspects of this complex issue and have developed promising models for us to analyze, choose from, and, where appropriate, replicate. The DOJ and Health and Human Services (HHS)-funded Elder Justice Roadmap provides a strategic planning resource developed by the field, for the field, to inform those efforts.

Chapter 4

Planning for Illness

*from a report by the **Securities and Exchange Commission's Office of Investor Education and Advocacy** and the **Consumer Financial Protection Bureau's Office for Older Americans***

"Diminished financial capacity" is a term used to describe a decline in a person's ability to manage money and financial assets to serve his or her best interests, including the inability to understand the consequences of investment decisions.

While the inability to manage one's money is clearly a problem in itself, when people of any age lose the capability to manage their finances, they may also become more vulnerable to investment fraud and other forms of financial abuse.

Preparing for your own financial future: Hope for the best, but plan for the worst.

Losing the ability to manage your finances may be something you'd rather not think about. We often think about our financial capabilities, like our ability to drive, as an important measure of our independence. But planning ahead may help you stay in control of your finances, even if diminished financial capacity becomes a serious problem. Taking the steps listed below now may help avoid or minimize problems for you and your family.

Organize your important documents

Organize and store important documents in a safe, easily accessible location. That way, they are readily available in an emergency. Give copies to trusted loved ones or let them know where to find the documents. Typically, the following documents will be most relevant to your finances:

§ Insurance policies
§ Pension and other retirement benefit summaries
§ Social Security payment information
§ Contact information for financial and medical professionals, such as doctors, lawyers, accountants, and securities professionals.

Bank and brokerage statements and account information.

Make a list of your accounts with account numbers. *Keep a separate list of online bank and brokerage passwords and PINs and keep the lists in a safe place.* In addition, make a list of the locations of your safe-deposit boxes, including where the keys to the safe-deposit boxes are located. Also, keep your recent bank and brokerage statements available, as well as information about how to get those statements online if you access them electronically.

Mortgage and credit information.

Make a list of your debts and regular payments, with account numbers and names of the financial institutions that issued the loans or credit cards.

The SEC's Office of Investor Education and Advocacy and the CFPB's Office for Older Americans offers the information in this chapter to help investors and consumers understand the potential impact of diminished capacity on their ability to make financial decisions and to encourage investors and consumers to plan for possible diminished financial capacity well before it happens.

Provide your financial professionals with trusted emergency contacts.

If you have a financial professional, such as a broker or investment adviser, provide that person with emergency or alternate contact information in case he or she cannot contact you or suspects something is wrong. You may wish to discuss with your financial professional what you would consider to be an "emergency," and specify when he or she may contact someone on your behalf.

Discuss what information can be shared with your emergency contact.

For example, you might provide your financial professional with a simple written instruction, such as: "Please call my son Mark at (222) 555–5555 if: (i) you are unable to reach me and there appears to be unusual activity regarding my account; (ii) you are unable to reach me for two weeks irrespective of any unusual account activity; or (iii) if you think I am confused or acting strangely." Providing an emergency contact generally will not enable the person to make investment decisions on your behalf—so be sure to take other steps if you want someone else to manage your accounts if you cannot.

Consider creating a durable financial power of attorney.

A financial power of attorney gives someone the legal authority to make financial decisions for you if you cannot. That person is called your agent. The document is called "durable" because it remains in effect even if you become incapacitated. You retain the ability to change it or cancel it as long as you are still able to make decisions. A financial power of attorney differs from a health care power of attorney, which only covers health care decisions. You may want to consult with a lawyer to determine whether a durable financial power of attorney is right for you.

After signing a durable financial power of attorney, you can still manage your money and property as long as you have the ability to make decisions. Also, it is important to remember that you always have the option to change who you choose to act as your appointed representative and the individuals you allow to access your financial information. *As you are essentially giving financial decision-making authority to your agent, it is critical that he or she be someone you can trust.*

Think about involving a trusted relative, friend, or professional.

Besides listing them as emergency contacts, you may wish to give a trusted relative, friend, or professional an overview of your finances (even if you don't want to share all the details). For example, you might ask your broker or bank to send duplicate statements to your daughter or accountant. You might also consider asking a trusted friend or relative to join you on periodic visits to your financial professional. This would give someone you trust a sense of your financial situation and with whom you've been doing business. *If you choose to involve a relative or friend, it is very important it is someone you are sure you can trust. Consider discussing the selection of the person with a number of other trusted friends or relatives.*

Keep things up to date.

Be sure that if something changes (for example, you open a new account) you keep your information as current as possible. Also, your trusted contact may change over time. Keep your financial professionals informed of changes regarding who has authority to review your account or whom they should contact in case of an emergency.

Speak up if something goes wrong.

If you ever think someone is taking advantage of you, or that you've been the victim of a fraud, *speak up*. Sadly, sometimes even financial professionals and people we know commit financial crimes.

There's no shame in being a victim, and the sooner you let someone know about it, the better chance there is of putting an end to it. Contact information for reporting abuse appears at the end of this document.

Helping others who may have diminished financial capacity

You may have a parent or other loved one with diminished financial capacity, or who you worry may face that issue in the future. If so, consider the following steps to help.

Have an open conversation about investments and other financial matters sooner rather than later.

Even if it feels awkward, it is important to have an honest conversation about finances. Ask your loved one to consider taking the steps outlined above. Even if he or she does not want to take these steps, ask your relative or friend to consider how he or she wants to maintain control of his or her finances in the future. Explain that advance planning is a way to make sure that a trusted person makes decisions if he or she no longer can.

Help your relative or friend with managing finances.

You may also offer to take a more active role in helping your loved one manage his or her financial accounts. Be alert both to mistakes that your loved one may make in managing finances and to any signs of elder financial abuse.

It can be hard to tell whether actions are the result of confusion or of financial exploitation. For example, if you find that a loved one has paid the same bill twice by mistake, you should help him or her fix the error. But beware that multiple or unusual payments could also be a sign of financial exploitation, so don't rule out that possibility without looking into it. Be on guard for any sudden changes in investments that seem out of keeping with the loved one's longstanding goals, values, and investment style. These changes may have come about because of confusion or may be a sign of financial exploitation.

If your family member or friend has named you to manage money or property, understand your responsibilities and how you can protect your loved one from financial exploitation. For example, your loved one may have named you as an agent under a power of attorney or a trustee under a revocable living trust. Read the Consumer Financial Protection Bureau's *Managing Someone Else's Money* guides. They walk you through your duties, tell you how to watch out for financial exploitation and scams, and tell you where you can go for help.

Financial steps to take

If you've been asked by a loved one or friend to help out with his or her finances, here are some things you can do to help:

Help with ongoing financial responsibilities.

You may need to take on immediate tasks, such as helping to pay bills, arranging for benefit claims, preparing tax returns, or helping with investment decisions.

Review their investment portfolio.

This might be a good time to help reevaluate the person's portfolio in light of his or her financial and medical situation. Does the person expect a big increase in health care, personal care, or other costs as a result of his or her illness or disability? If so, will he or she have enough cash or liquid assets on hand to cover those costs? (Liquid investments are assets that the owner can sell readily and without paying a hefty fee to get money when it is needed.)

These can be complex questions and you may wish to discuss them with a financial professional. Keep in mind that buying and selling investments on behalf of a loved one requires legal authority, through a power of attorney, a trust, or similar arrangement.

Assess the riskiness of their investment portfolio.

All investments involve some level of risk. But do the investments present the right level of risk at this stage of the person's life? If not, you may wish to consider contacting a registered investment adviser representative or registered broker-dealer representative for help.

Contact their investment professional.

If your loved one has a financial professional and has authorized that person to speak with you, make the professional aware of your loved one's condition. This is critical so that the financial professional can make recommendations appropriate to the client's financial needs and can watch for signs of declining financial skills or potential abuse.

Your financial professional, or that of your loved one, may raise topics discussed here. Financial services firms are paying increasing attention to improving communications on this subject. If a financial professional does not raise these topics, however, you should feel free to raise them yourself.

Additional Resources

Financial Protection for Older Americans webpage of the Consumer Financial Protection Bureau (CFPB), available at consumerfinance. gov/older-americans

The US Department of Justice's Elder Justice Initiative website at justice.gov/elderjustice/ (including the page on victim and family support)

The SEC Investor.gov web page for seniors, available at investor. gov/seniors

To report suspected elder abuse in general, locate the appropriate adult protective services agency by calling the Eldercare Locator at (800) 677–1116, or see eldercare.gov.

Elder financial abuse often violates one or more criminal laws. To report it, contact your local police or sheriff.

To report suspected elder financial abuse involving brokers or investment advisers, contact:

- The SEC at (800) 732–0330 or sec.gov/complaint/select .shtml, or
- The Financial Industry Regulatory Authority (FINRA) Securities Helpline for seniors at (844) 574–3577 or www.nra.org /investors/investor-complaint-center, or

- Your state securities regulator. For a contact list of state securities regulators, visit nasaa.org/about-us/contact-us/contact -your-regulator.

The SEC's Office of Investor Education and Advocacy and the CFPB's Office of Older Americans have provided information for this chapter as a service to investors and consumers. It is neither a legal interpretation nor a statement of SEC or CFPB policy. If you have questions concerning the meaning or application of a particular law or rule, please consult with an attorney who specializes in securities or consumer finance law.

Chapter 5

Top 10 Scams on the Elderly

*from a report by the **US Senate Special Committee on Aging***

The US Senate Special Committee on Aging has identified these top ten types of fraud complaints committed against senior citizens in the United States:

1. IRS Impersonation Scam

The Treasury Inspector General for Tax Administration (TIGTA) has called the Internal Revenue Service (IRS) impersonation scam "the largest, most pervasive impersonation scam in the history of the IRS." According to TIGTA, nearly 900,000 Americans have been targeted by scammers impersonating IRS officials, with 12,000 to 13,000 people submitting complaints on this scam every week as of December 2015. Additionally, 30 to 50 people a week reported that they lost money to the scam; more than 5,000 Americans have lost a total of at least $26 million via this scam. The IRS impersonation scam was the most frequent scam reported to the Fraud Hotline in 2015.

While there are multiple variations of the IRS impersonation scam, criminals generally accuse victims of owing back taxes and penalties. They then threaten retaliation, such as home foreclosure, arrest, and, in some cases, deportation, if immediate payment is not made by a certified check, credit card, electronic wire-transfer, or pre-paid debit card. Victims are told that if they immediately pay the amount that is allegedly owed, the issue with the IRS will be resolved and the arrest warrant, or other adverse action, will be cancelled.

Once victims make an initial payment, they will often be told that further review of their tax records has indicated another discrepancy and that they must pay an additional sum of money to resolve that difference or else face arrest or other adverse action. Scammers will often take victims through this process multiple times. As long as the victims remain hooked, the scammers will tell them they owe more money.

These scam calls most often involve a disguised, or "spoofed," caller identification (caller ID) number to make the victims believe that the call is coming from the "202" area code, the area code for Washington, DC, where the US Department of the Treasury and the IRS are headquartered. In a recent variation of this scam, calls also appear to be coming from the "509," "206," and "306" area codes, all Washington State area codes.

Scammers have also been known to "spoof" their phone numbers to make it appear as though they are calling from a local law enforcement agency. When the unsuspecting victims see the "Internal Revenue Service" or the name of the local police department appear on their caller IDs, they are understandably concerned and are often willing to follow the supposed government official's instructions in order to resolve the alleged tax issue.

"With such scams reaching epidemic proportions across the country, the IRS has released several tips to help taxpayers identify suspicious calls that may be part of a scam:

- The IRS will never call a taxpayer to demand immediate payment, nor will the agency call about taxes owed without first having mailed a bill to the taxpayer.
- The IRS will never demand that a taxpayer pay taxes without giving him or her the opportunity to question or appeal the amount claimed to be owed.
- The IRS will never ask for a credit or debit card number over the phone.
- The IRS will not threaten to send local police or other law enforcement to have a taxpayer arrested.
- The IRS will never require a taxpayer to use a specific payment method for taxes, such as a prepaid debit card."

Source: https://www.irs.gov/uac/Five-Easy-Ways-to-Spot-a-Scam-Phone Call

2. Sweepstakes Scams

Sweepstakes scams continue to claim senior victims who believe they have won a lottery and only need to take a few actions to obtain their winnings. Scammers will generally contact victims by phone or through the mail to tell them that they have won or have been entered to win a prize. Scammers then require the victims to pay a fee to either collect their supposed winnings or improve their odds of winning the prize. According to the Federal Trade Commission (FTC), the number of sweepstakes scams increased by 5.68% between 2013 and 2014. Sweepstakes scams start with a simple phone call, usually from a number beginning with "876," the country code for Jamaica. At first glance, this country code looks similar to a call coming from a toll-free American number. Scammers tell the victims that they have won the Jamaican lottery or a brand new car and that they must wire a few hundred dollars for upfront processing fees or taxes for their winnings to be delivered. Often, the criminals will instruct their victims not to share the good news with anyone so that it will be a "surprise" when their families find out. Scammers tell victims to send the money in a variety of ways, including prepaid debit cards, electronic wire transfers, money orders, and even cash.

Of course, no such winnings are ever delivered, and the "winners" get nothing but more phone calls, sometimes 50 to 100 calls per day, from scammers demanding additional money. Behind these calls is an organized and sophisticated criminal enterprise, overseeing boiler room operations in another country. Indeed, money scammed from victims helps fund organized crime in other parts of the world. Criminals once involved in narcotics trafficking have found these scams to be safer and more lucrative.

Expensive "lead lists" of potential victims are bought and sold by scammers to help find their targets. Satellite maps are used to locate and describe victims' homes to make the callers appear familiar with the community. Elaborate networks for the transfer of funds are established to evade the anti-fraud systems of financial institutions. Should victims move or change their phone numbers, the con artists use all of the technology at their disposal to reestablish contact.

The con artists adopt a variety of identities to keep the money coming in ever-increasing amounts. Some spend hours on the phone convincing seniors that they care deeply for them. Victims who resist their entreaties begin receiving calls from foreigners posing as American government officials, including local law enforcement, the Federal Bureau of Investigation (FBI), the Social Security Administration, and the Department of Homeland Security, asking for personal data and bank account numbers so that they can "solve" the crime.

3. Robocalls/Unwanted Phone Calls

In 2003, Congress passed legislation creating the national Do-Not-Call registry with the goal of putting an end to the plague of telemarketers who were interrupting Americans at all hours of the day with unwanted calls. Unfortunately, more than a decade after the registry was implemented, Americans are still being disturbed by telemarketers and scammers who ignore the Do-Not-Call registry and increasingly use robocall technology. Robocalling is the process of using equipment to mechanically, as opposed to manually, dial phone numbers in sequence. Robodialers can be used to distribute pre-recorded messages or to connect the person who answers the call with a live person.

Robocalls often originate offshore. Con artists usually spoof the number from which they are calling to either mask their true identity or take on a new identity. As described in the previous section on IRS impersonation scams, fraudsters spoof their numbers to make victims believe they are calling from the government or another legitimate entity. In addition, scammers will often spoof numbers to appear as if they are calling from the victims' home states or local area codes.

These robocalls have become an increasing nuisance to consumers in recent years due to advances in technology. Phone calls used to be routed through equipment that was costly and complicated to operate, which made high-volume calling from international locations difficult and expensive. This traditional, or legacy, equipment sent calls in analog format over a copper wire network and could not easily spoof a caller ID. Today, phone calls can be digitized and routed from anywhere in the world at practically no cost. This is done using Voice over Internet Protocol (VoIP) technology, which sends voice communications over the Internet. Robocalling allows scammers to maximize the number of individuals and households they can reach.

Many companies now offer third-party spoofing and robo-dialing services. Third-party spoofing companies provide an easy-to-use computer interface or cell phone app that allows calls to be spoofed at a negligible cost. To demonstrate how accessible this technology is, a staff member from the Special Committee on Aging spoofed two separate calls to Chairman Susan Collins during a Committee hearing on June 10, 2015, titled "Ringing Off the Hook: Examining the Proliferation of Unwanted Calls." By using an inexpensive smart phone app, the staff member was able to make it appear that the calls were from the IRS and the Department of Justice, respectively. The hearing examined why so many Americans are constantly receiving unsolicited calls even though they are on the national Do-Not-Call registry, discussed how advances in telephone technology makes it easier for scammers to cast a wide net and increase the number of potential victims they can reach, and highlighted possible technological solutions to this menace.

In response to the high volume of robo-calls that are made in violation of the national Do-Not-Call registry, the FTC launched a contest in October 2012 to identify innovative solutions to protect consumers from these calls. In April 2013, they announced that Nomorobo, a free service that screens and blocks robocalls made to VoIP phone numbers, was one of two winners of the their Robocall Challenge. Once a consumer registers his or her phone number, Nomorobo reroutes all incoming phone calls to a server that instantly checks the caller against a whitelist of legitimate callers and a blacklist of spammers. If the caller is on the whitelist, the phone continues to ring, but if the number is on the blacklist, the call will disconnect after one ring. Fraud hotline investigators have referred callers to the Nomorobo website and have received positive feedback from those who chose to register for the service.

The Federal Communications Commission (FCC) has published the following warnings for consumers to avoid being deceived by caller-ID spoofing:

"You may not be able to tell right away if an incoming call is spoofed. Be careful about responding to ANY request for personal identifying information.

- Never give out personal information such as account numbers, Social Security numbers, mother's maiden names, passwords, or other identifying information in response to unexpected calls or if you are at all suspicious.
- If you get an inquiry from someone who says they represent a company or a government agency seeking personal information, hang up and call the phone number on your account statement, in the phone book, or on the company's or government agency's website to verify the authenticity of the request.
- Use caution if you are being pressured for information immediately.
- If you have a voice mail account with your phone service, be sure to set a password for it. Some voicemail services are preset to allow access if you call in from your own phone number. A hacker could spoof your home phone number and gain access to your voice mail if you do not set a password."

Source: fcc.gov/cgb/consumerfacts/callerid.pdf

4. Computer Scams

The Aging Committee saw an increase in the frequency and severity of computer-based scams in 2015. Private industry has seen a similar increase in the prevalence of this scam: Microsoft reported receiving more than 180,000 consumer complaints of computer-based fraud between May 2014 and October 2015. The company estimated that 3.3 million Americans are victims of technical support scams annually, with losses of roughly $1.5 billion per year. Unlike other victim-assisted frauds, where the scammers are successful in just one out of a hundred-plus attempts, it appears that computer-based scams have a very high success rate. In addition, in 2014, the Internet Crime Complaint Center (IC3), a partnership between the FBI and the National White Collar Crime Center, received 269,492 computer fraud complaints with a loss of $800,492,073. Americans age 60 and older accounted for 16.57% of these complaints.

The basic scam involves con artists trying to gain victims' trust by pretending to be associated with a well-known technology company, such as Microsoft, Apple, or Dell. They then falsely claim that the victims' computers have been infected with a virus. Con artists convince victims to give them remote access to their computers, personal information, and credit card and bank account numbers so that victims can be "reimbursed" for fraudulent charges stemming from the virus. In a related scam, individuals surfing the Internet may see a pop-up window on their computer instructing them to contact a tech-support agent. Sometimes, scammers have used the pop-up window to hack into victims' computers, lock them out, and require victims to pay a ransom to regain control of their computers. Below are several of the most common variations of this scam:

- Scammers Contact Victims. In the most prevalent variation of this scam, con artists randomly call potential victims and offer to clean their computers and/or sell them a long term or technical support "service." The con artists usually direct victims' computers to display benign error messages that appear on every computer to convince victims that their computers are malfunctioning. Scammers generally charge victims between $150 and $800 and may install free programs or trial versions of antivirus programs to give the illusion that they are repairing victims' computers. If victims express concern about the price, the con artists will often entice victims to pay by offering a "senior citizen discount."

- Victims Unknowingly Contact Scammers. Some consumers unknowingly call a fraudulent tech support number after viewing the phone number online. Consumers who search for tech support online may see the number for the scammer at the top of their "sponsored results." The FTC found that a network of scammers paid Google more than one million dollars since 2010 for advertisements and for certain key search terms. Some key search terms included: "virus removal," "how to get rid of a computer virus," "McAfee Customer Support," and "Norton Support." These search terms are cleverly chosen to confuse the consumer into thinking the fraudsters are associated with well-known companies. Other fraudsters use pop-up messages on consumers' computer screens that direct potential victims to call them.

- Ransomware. Scammers use malware or spyware to infect victims' computers with a virus or encrypt the computers so they cannot be used until a fee is paid. If victims refuse to pay, scammers will render the computer useless, prompting the appearance of a blue screen that can only be removed with a password known by the scammers. The fraud hotline has received reports that scammers sometimes admit to victims that it is a scam and refuse to unlock the victims' computers unless a "ransom" payment is made.

- Fraudulent Refund. Scammers contact victims stating they are owed a refund for prior services. The scammers generally convince victims to provide them with access to their computers to process an online wire transfer. Instead of refunding the money, however, the fraudsters use the victims' account information to charge the consumers.

The FTC has responded to computer-based scams through law enforcement actions and ongoing investigations. In 2014, the agency brought action against six firms based primarily in India that were responsible for stealing more than $100 million from thousands of victims.

> **Tips from the FTC to help consumers avoid becoming a victim of a computer-based scam**
>
> "If you get a call from someone who claims to be a tech support person, hang up and call the company yourself on a phone number you know to be genuine. A caller who creates a sense of urgency or uses high-pressure tactics is probably a scam artist.
> Keep these other tips in mind:
>
> - Don't give control of your computer to a third party who calls you out of the blue.
> - Do not rely on caller ID alone to authenticate a caller. Criminals spoof caller ID numbers. They may appear to be calling from a legitimate company or a local number, when they're not even in the same country as you.
> - Online search results might not be the best way to find technical support or get a company's

contact information. Scammers sometimes place online ads to convince *you* to call *them*. They pay to boost their ranking in search results so their websites and phone numbers appear above those of legitimate companies. If you want tech support, look for a company's contact information on their software package or on your receipt.

- Never provide your credit card or financial information to someone who calls and claims to be from tech support.
- If a caller pressures you to buy a computer security product or says there is a subscription fee associated with the call, hang up. If you're concerned about your computer, call your security software company directly and ask for help.
- Never give your password on the phone. No legitimate organization calls you and asks for your password.
- Put your phone number on the National Do Not Call Registry, and then report illegal sales calls."

Source: https://www.consumer.ftc.gov/articles/0346-tech-support-scams

5. Identity Theft

Identity theft has been the Federal Trade Commission's (FTC) most common consumer complaint for the past 15 years, with 212,698 Americans reporting being victimized in 2014 alone. Nearly 40% of the identity theft complaints that the FTC received in 2014 were reported by consumers age 50 and older.

Identity thieves not only disrupt the lives of individuals by draining bank accounts, making unauthorized credit card charges, and damaging credit reports, but they also often defraud the government and taxpayers by using stolen personal information to submit fraudulent billings to Medicare or Medicaid or to apply for and receive Social Security benefits to which they are not entitled. Fraudsters also use stolen personal information, including Social Security numbers (SSNs), to commit tax fraud or to fraudulently apply for jobs and earn wages. According to the FTC, government documents/benefits fraud was the most common type of identity theft reported by consumers in 2014, comprising 38.7% of all identity theft complaints.

Tax-related identity theft continues to disrupt the lives of Americans. The growing use of commercial tax filing software and online tax filing services has led to opportunities for thieves to commit fraud without stealing SSNs. In some cases, thieves can illegally access an existing customer's account simply by entering that individual's username, e-mail address, or name and correctly guessing the password. This is often referred to as an "account takeover." Whether the thief uses this method to access an existing account or uses stolen personal information to create a new account, the end result is often the same: early in the tax filing season, the thief files a false tax return using a victim's identity and directs the refund to his own mailing address or bank account. The victim only discovers this theft when he files his own return and the IRS refuses to accept it because a refund has already been issued. In November 2015, the IRS reversed a long-standing policy and now will provide victims with copies of the fake returns upon written request. The documents will provide victims with details to help them discover how much of their personal information was stolen.

Medical identity theft occurs when someone steals personal information—an individual's name, SSN, or health insurance claim number (HICN)—to obtain medical care, buy prescription drugs, or submit fake billings to Medicare. Medical identity theft can disrupt lives, damage credit ratings, and waste taxpayer dollars. Some identity thieves even use stolen personal information to obtain medical care for themselves or others, putting lives at risk if the theft is not detected and the wrong information ends up in the victims' medical files. Claims for services or items obtained with stolen HICNs might be included in the beneficiary's Medicare billing history and could delay or prevent the beneficiary from receiving needed services until the discrepancy is resolved.

In April 2015, President Obama signed a law that requires the Centers for Medicare & Medicaid Services (CMS) to remove SSNs from Medicare cards by 2019. On October 7, 2015, the Aging Committee held a hearing titled, "Protecting Seniors from Identity Theft: Is the Federal Government Doing Enough?" The Committee heard testimony from the CMS official in charge of implementing the Medicare card replacement process and from the Health and Human Services Office of Inspector General about investigative efforts to combat medical identity theft.

Tips to Help Secure Your Identity

- Medicare and Social Security will not call you to ask for your bank information or SSN.
- There will never be a fee charged to obtain a Social Security or Medicare card.
- Never give out personal information over the phone.
- Sensitive personal and financial documents should be kept secure at all times.
- Review all medical bills to spot any services that you didn't receive.

What to Do if You Suspect You are a Victim of Identity Theft
What to Do Right Away
- Call the companies where you know the fraud occurred.
- Place a fraud alert with a credit reporting agency and get your credit report from one of the three national credit bureaus.
- Report identity theft to the FTC.
- File a report with your local police department.

What to Do Next:
- Close new accounts opened in your name.
- Remove bogus charges from your accounts.
- Correct your credit report.
- Consider adding an extended fraud alert or credit freeze.

6. Grandparent Scams

A common scam that deliberately targets older Americans is the "grandparent scam." In this scam, imposters either pretend to be the victim's grandchild or claim to be with the victim's grandchild. The fraudsters claim the grandchild is in trouble and needs money to help with an emergency, such as getting out of jail, paying a hospital bill, or leaving a foreign country. Scammers play on victims' emotions and trick concerned grandparents into wiring money to them. Once the money is wired, it is difficult to trace.

In another version of the scam, instead of the "grandchild" making the phone call, the con artist pretends to be an arresting police officer, a lawyer, or a doctor. It is also common for con artists impersonating victims' grandchildren to talk briefly with the victims and then hand the phone over to an accomplice impersonating an authority figure. This gives the scammers' stories more credibility and reduces the chance that the victims will recognize that the voice on the phone does not belong to their grandchild.

In 2014, the FTC received 14,521 complaints of individuals impersonating friends and family members, up from 11,793 in 2012. Between January 1, 2012, and May 31, 2014, individuals reported more than $42 million in losses to the FTC from scams involving the impersonation of family members and friends.

To help your loved one avoid this type of scam, make sure all family members agree on a "password" that can be requested by either party to confirm your identity over the phone. Asking for the name of the family pet, for instance, would be a way for any senior to be sure they are really speaking with a loving relative.

7. Elder Financial Abuse

Financial exploitation of older Americans is the illegal or improper use of an older adult's funds, property, or assets. According to MetLife's Mature Market Institute, in 2010 seniors lost an estimated $2.9 billion because of financial exploitation, $300 million more than the year before, although these numbers are likely substantially underreported. One study found that, for every case of financial fraud that is reported, as many as 14 go unreported. A 2011 Government Accountability Office (GAO) study found that approximately 14.1% of adults age 60 and older experienced physical, psychological, or sexual abuse; potential neglect; or financial exploitation in the past year.

The fraud hotline documents complaints of elder abuse and refers callers to Adult Protective Services (APS) for further action. APS employees receive reports of alleged abuse, investigate these allegations, determine whether or not the alleged abuse can be substantiated, and arrange for services to ensure victims' well-being. APS can also refer cases to law enforcement agencies or district attorneys for criminal investigation and prosecution. APS workers ideally coordinate with local law enforcement and prosecutors to take legal action, but the effectiveness of this relationship can vary significantly from state to state. As of 2015, every state has an elder abuse statute.

Older Americans are particularly vulnerable to financial exploitation because financial decision-making ability can decrease with age. One study found that women are almost twice as likely to be victims of financial abuse. Most victims are between the ages of 80 and 89, live alone, and require support with daily activities. Perpetrators include family members, paid home care workers; those with fiduciary responsibilities, such as financial advisors or legal guardians, or strangers who defraud older adults through mail, telephone, or Internet scams.

One of the provisions of the Elder Justice Act of 2009, which was enacted in 2010, seeks to improve the federal response to this issue. The law formed the Elder Justice Coordinating Council, which first convened on October 11, 2012 and is tasked with increasing cooperation among federal agencies. Experts agree that multidisciplinary teams that bring together professionals from various fields such as social work, medicine, law, nursing, and the financial industry can expedite and resolve complex cases, identify systemic problems, and raise awareness about emerging scams.

While some states have laws that require financial professionals to report suspected financial exploitation of seniors to the appropriate local or state authorities, there currently is no federal requirement to do so. Some financial professionals may fail to report suspected financial exploitation due to a lack of training or fear of repercussions for violating privacy laws. In October 2015, Aging Committee Chairman Susan Collins and Ranking Member Claire McCaskill introduced the *Senior $afe Act of 2015*, which would provide certain individuals with immunity for disclosing suspected financial exploitation of senior citizens. The Financial Industry Regulatory Authority is simultaneously pursuing rule-making that would empower financial professionals to protect their senior clients from financial abuse.

Some localities with large senior populations have established special units to address elder abuse, including elder financial abuse. In October 2015, prosecutors in Montgomery County, Maryland, successfully brought charges against an individual who, over several years, embezzled more than $400,000 before one of the victim's bankers discovered suspicious activity in his account and alerted APS. The fraudster had convinced the victim to give her power of attorney and control over his finances. She was sentenced to five years in jail for financial exploitation of a vulnerable adult, theft, and embezzlement.

The Aging Committee has brought to light many schemes that have defrauded seniors out of their hard-earned retirement savings. It is deeply troubling when a senior falls victim to one of these schemes, but it is even more egregious when the perpetrator is a family member, caregiver, or trusted financial adviser.

8. Grant Scams

Grant scams, of which there are multiple variations, are frequently reported to the Aging Committee's Fraud Hotline. In the most common version of this scam, consumers receive an unsolicited phone call from con artists claiming that they are from the "Federal Grants Administration" or the "Federal Grants Department"—agencies that do not exist. In another version of this scam, scammers place advertisements in the classified section of local newspapers offering "free grants." Scammers will request that victims wire money for processing fees or taxes before the money can be sent to them.

The Federal Trade Commission (FTC) defines grant scams as "deceptive practices by businesses or individuals marketing either government grant opportunities or financial aid assistance services; problems with student loan processors, debt collectors collecting on defaulted student loans, diploma mills, and other unaccredited educational institutions; etc." According to FTC data, the frequency of Americans reporting grant scams has dropped over the past three years. In 2014, the FTC received 8,032 complaints, which was about a 10% decrease from the prior year.

The National Consumers League has published the following tips for consumers to avoid falling victim to a federal grant scam:

- Do not give out your bank account information to anyone you do not know. Scammers pressure people to divulge their bank account information so that they can steal the money in the account. Do not share bank account information unless you are familiar with the company and know why the information is necessary.
- Government grants are made for specific purposes, not just because someone is a good taxpayer. They also require an application process; they are not simply given over the phone. Most government grants are awarded to states, cities, schools, and nonprofit organizations to help provide services or fund research projects. Grants to individuals are typically for things like college expenses or disaster relief.
- Government grants never require fees of any kind. You might have to provide financial information to prove that you qualify for a government grant, but you never have to pay to get one.

Source: http://www.nclnet.org

9. Romance Scams/Confidence Fraud

More and more Americans are turning to the Internet for dating. As of December 2013, one in 10 American adults had used online dating services, and online dating is now a $2 billion industry. As Americans increasingly turn to online dating to find love, con artists are following suit—not for love, but for money. In 2014, the Aging Committee's Fraud Hotline began receiving reports from individuals regarding romance scams. Sometimes these reports were not just from seniors, but also from friends and family members whose loved ones were deeply involved in a fictitious cyber-relationship. This is one of the most heartbreaking scams because con artists exploit seniors' loneliness and vulnerability.

Typically, scammers contact victims online, through either a chatroom, dating site, social media site, or email. According to the Federal Bureau of Investigation's (FBI) Internet Crime Complaint Center (IC3), 12% of the complaints submitted in 2014 contained a social media aspect. Con artists have been known to create elaborate profile pages, giving their fabricated story more credibility. Con artists often call and chat on the phone to prove that they are real. These conversations can take place over weeks and even months as the con artists build trust with their victims. In some instances, con artists have even promised to marry their victims.

Inevitably, con artists in these scams will ask their victims for money for a variety of things. Often the con artists will ask for travel expenses so they can visit the victims in the United States. In other cases, they claim to need money for medical emergencies, hotel bills, hospital bills for a child or other relative, visas or other official documents, or losses from a temporary financial setback. Unfortunately, in spite of telling their victims they will never ask for any more money, something always comes up resulting in the con artists requesting more money.

In 2014, the FBI's IC3 received more than 5,883 complaints about romance and confidence scams that cost victims $86.7 million dollars. Nearly half of these victims were age 50 or older, and this group accounted for approximately 70% of the money lost to this scam last year. Romance and confidence scams disproportionally target women, usually between the ages of 30 and 55 years old. Unfortunately, both the amount of financial loss and the number of complaints for this crime have increased in recent years.

Tips from the FBI's IC3 to help prevent victims from falling victim to romance scams:

- Be cautious of individuals who claim the romance was destiny or fate, or that you are meant to be together.
- Be cautious if an individual tells you he or she is in love with you and cannot live without you but needs you to send money to fund a visit.
- Fraudsters typically claim to be originally from the United States (or your local region), but are currently overseas, or going overseas, for business or family matters.

Source: https://www.fbi.gov/news/news_blog/2014-ic3-annual-report

10. Home Improvement Scam

The last of the top 10 scams reported to the fraud hotline in 2015 were home improvement scams. There are several variations of this scam in which scammers show up at victims' doors and offer to perform a service for a price that seems fair. These service jobs frequently involve, but are not limited to, repairing a roof, repaving a driveway, repainting

FTC's Tips on How Tell if a Contractor Might Not Be Reputable
Don't do business with someone who:

- Claims that "the deal is good for today only." Often, con artists will pressure you for an immediate decision by telling you that, if you wait even another day, they cannot guarantee the same price.
- Lacks professionalism. Ask if the person has a business card, or check to see if the person's vehicle is marked with a company logo or information.
- Only accepts cash; asks you to pay everything, or a sizeable deposit, upfront; or tells you to borrow money from a lender the contractor knows.
- Is not licensed. Many states, but not all, require contractors to be licensed and/or bonded. Check with your local building department or consumer protection agency to learn about licensing requirements in your area.
- States that he "just happens to have materials left over from a previous job" or "just happens to be in the area."

Source: https://www.consumer.ftc.gov/blog/home-improvement
-scams-are-no-laughing-matter

a house or room, or installing a home security system. The contractors usually ask for immediate payment in advance but then do substandard work, or no work at all. Seniors, those who live alone, individuals with disabilities, and victims of weather-related disasters are common targets.

Home improvement scams occur frequently during a change of season. Con artists will often take advantage of the warmer weather, or approaching cooler weather, and use it as an opportunity to convince victims that it is the perfect time to get home improvement jobs done. In 2014, the Federal Trade Commission (FTC) received 8,327 complaints about home repair, improvement, and product scams.

Scammers will also frequently target individuals who have been affected by a recent weather-related disaster. Con artists may appear after a storm, promising to help with immediate clean-up and debris removal. For instance, after a flood, these scammers may tell victims that they can restore their appliances or haul away damaged items for a fee. Scammers then demand immediate payment for work that they will never do. Unlicensed and unskilled contractors may also offer to restore damaged homes and then fail to do the work or do a substandard job. Since flooding can cause lasting problems, such as mold, it's important that homeowners verify that any company they are considering to clean or repair their homes has the proper licenses, insurance, and experience to do the job.

PART 2

TAKING ACTION

Chapter 6

If You Suspect Abuse: How to Report a Problem

by Tom Coleman

Thomas F. Coleman *is an attorney who, for more than four decades, has been advocating for equal rights and pursuing justice for populations who have historically been subject to unjust discrimination. Beneficiaries of his advocacy have included gays and lesbians, single people, nontraditional families, troubled teenagers, and people with disabilities. His efforts have taken him from local courts to state supreme courts to the nation's highest court, and from city halls to state capitols to the halls of Congress. He has used print and broadcast media in public education campaigns to promote his causes. Coleman's most recent project focuses on protecting the rights of seniors and people with developmental disabilities who become ensnared in broken and dysfunctional state guardianship systems. More information about his career and current activities can be found at* www.tomcoleman.us.

I f you know someone who is being isolated or abused, financially or otherwise, what can you as an individual do to protect them, specifically?

Even though you may have learned to recognize isolation and abuse, what are the practical steps you can take to protect your loved one—or anyone for that matter?

What should you do? What can you do?

Document the problem

First, the most important thing is to **document** what is happening in whatever way you're able to document it. When you eventually reach out to somebody for help (the sooner the better!)—whether it's the police or APS (Adult Protective Services), an attorney, a member of the clergy, or anyone else—they do not want to hear a rambling emotional story that leaves them without any facts to act upon. They may not have time to listen to a disorganized jumble of feelings and complaints, or their incentive may be to get you off the phone and move on because they have an immense caseload and too many problems to deal with already.

Be aware of the fact that you're in charge. You're the person who is going to have to see this through. You can't just pick up the phone, make a call, and walk away, assuming that everything is going to happen automatically on its own.

Monitor progress

You are going to have to monitor the progress of whatever complaint you make no matter what agency or authority you're appealing to. You are going to want to lead this rescue mission every step of the way. So realize that you are it: the buck stops with you. If you don't do it, it ain't going to happen. Be aware of that and be prepared for the long haul however long it takes.

Do not make any assumptions other than knowing that whatever can go wrong along the way, it probably will go wrong. You need to be watchful and to record your observations at all times. You need to write this up or make a video or recording of some kind—document in whatever way you can what's happening. Whatever you want to do, whatever works best for you. But you need to have the facts.

The facts are not the whole rambling story. You can embellish later if you want, but the simplest facts come first: Who is the victim? Name, address, phone number, and whatever other identifying information you have about them. Think about what someone will specifically need to follow up.

Make a list

How are you related to this? What exactly do you believe has been happening to this victim? Make a list. They're being isolated. They're not being allowed to see who they want to see. Or someone is tapping into their bank account.

These are typical complaints so you need not feel guilt, fear, or shame in reporting them.

So make a factual list and include buzzwords—a phrase or a sentence to sound the alarm. You can explain in greater detail later what is most significant to you personally, but the word *isolation* should trigger a response—"They're being isolated from me, from all their friends." Or maybe they're being overmedicated much of the time. They're groggy, unable to respond. There is money missing, surreptitious theft as a form of financial abuse.

Assign a **title** to each one of your complaints. Describe it briefly in maybe two sentences, in a form someone can readily understand. When did it start? Has it been ongoing? During what dates has it been occurring?

If they've been physically assaulted, how did you find out? Did you hear screams? How long ago? On what dates?

Now add some other details. What additional evidence is there? Who besides you knows about this? Are you the only witness? If so, why should anyone believe you? Who else can corroborate your version of events? Why should they take your word?

The care and preparation you take in presenting your case in a rational manner will go a long way to establishing your credibility. Try to condense the original complaint down to a single page or two—that's all of a summary that anybody in a position of authority, especially at first glance, can absorb or will need to read initially.

If you want to include other **attachments**, make a parenthetical notation, referring to Exhibit A or "see this letter" or "see other document."

The point is to make everything easy to read and easy to understand.

Get help from others

There's strength in numbers, so go to somebody else who you trust and have them review what you've prepared if you can. Feedback from someone you trust can be extremely valuable. Run it by them and have them read it. If they share your point of view and have had similar experiences, ask them to co-sign the documentation. Consider their suggestions and take encouragement from their energy and support. Remember: if it's not understandable to your best friend, it may not be understandable to a total stranger at a government agency.

Who will listen outside of family or friends? Where are you going to take this information? Be aware that any third-party person or agency—and even the victim—may deny the reality of the situation.

If you think the person you are concerned about might deny what you're saying (whether out of fear or for some other reason) explain that in a footnote or at the end of your story so you have a ready explanation for the investigator.

Denying or minimizing an abusive situation can be the default strategy of a confused or frightened victim. They're often afraid that revealing the abuse may only make matters worse.

You may need to reassure, shelter or, if possible, rapidly remove the victim from the situation as a matter of course. You may have to be extra strategic, give your options plenty of thought, and even prepare for a series of battles that may take place over many months, both inside and outside a courtroom.

Are you going to share details with others or just keep it within the family? Are you going to file a report with the police? With Adult Protective Services, or the sheriff? How about the victim's medical doctor?

Prepare for resistance

Be advised, however, that if some private company or governmental agency is a part of the problem, you may not want to share it with them.

If liability issues are at play for an entity, they may want to downplay it—to make it go away the way a school district may want to escape liability if they've ignored bullying or a teacher has been abusing you.

Ideally, make sure to go to someone who is not a party to the situation or who has no incentive to cover up the problem.

You might want to go to multiple agencies. For example, if you file it with the Adult Protective Services, cross-file it with the police and do so in writing, return receipt requested. The important thing is to document, document, document.

Remember that you're probably not going to be able to solve the main problem of systemic or secretive abuse on your own or it would have been solved already.

Therefore, it's always a good idea to reach out for support. Remember that asking for help is not a sign of weakness. Rather, it's the smart thing to do.

Because this could be a very long and rocky road, you may be going through personal strife and misery for months or years over this. You will always want to have at least one person on your side, who's on your team, who you can confide in, to give you emotional support—your own team to help you through. There's nothing wrong with that.

Escalate if needed

If you are not satisfied by the response to your formal complaint, be prepared to go higher and higher. If you need to, be prepared to **get political**.

You might go to your city council member, or someone on your Board of Supervisors, to announce that this abuse is occurring.

Now your complaint is not just about the original abuse, it's about the sheriff's department or the unresponsive labyrinth of Adult Protective Services.

The saddest part of any story is one that ends in a death. And, yes, that is a real concern and it happens all the time. This is yet another reason to take your rescue mission very seriously.

Please know that as a matter of course you can write directly to an elected official, to a newspaper or TV station, and you can even write directly to a judge. Ultimately, you may want to file a petition for a guardianship yourself.

You must not allow yourself to be stopped from letting someone in power know that a wrong is being committed. That is the only way to circumvent the worst possible outcome.

This may seem like a long and winding path, but it is in the end the only way to get the righteous relief you want for yourself and for your loved one.

Chapter 7

Working with Professionals

by Thomas Lee Wright

D octors and lawyers inevitably play an increasing role in our lives, during these uncertain times, especially in our latter years. In addition to competency in the practice of their skills, among other things, you and your loved one have a legitimate right to be treated ethically and with respect.

Ideally, your parents will have long-standing relationships with doctors and lawyers they've come to trust over time. Some may even have earned the right to be considered as if they are members of your immediate family. Such is the bond that can form between you and the professionals who handle the intimate and often complex hurdles that can arise in the legal and medical realms of life. In many cases, however, such relationships do not exist or have faded away over the years as the parties involved have grown older and reached retirement age.

No matter the circumstances, it is always best to check the background, credentials, and references of any professionals you will be employing to help you plan for your family's care, whether now or in the future. While the vast majority of those who've pursued careers in the law or in medicine are honest and competent, it is part of the mission of this book to remind the reader that there are those in the general population capable of abusing the elderly, whether intentionally or unintentionally, in every walk of life.

Keep in mind too that you will most likely need the professional guidance of a doctor in tandem with an attorney to track your parent's cognitive abilities from an established baseline of competency through a likely period of inevitable decline. You will want more than one person you can trust to watch out for your parent's best interests as well as your own.

If possible, make sure you have your own doctor and your own attorney to provide alternative options and opinions whenever there are difficult decisions to be made. You should avoid granting too much power and influence to any individual outside your family. If you find you have allowed any third party to become so autonomous and powerful in your life that they are keeping essential information from you and it's making you concerned and uncomfortable, you have unwittingly set up yourself and your parent for potential white-collar abuse in the legal or medical realm and it's time to hire a different professional advisor. Conflicts of interest among the professionals you hire should be identified and avoided at all cost as they may arise from time to time in the care and protection of your parents.

This chapter spells out some of the challenges both you and the professionals you employ will face while collaborating to protect your parents. It also addresses issues that may arise when you are hiring a doctor or a lawyer to become a member of your family team.

The Role of the Physician

Due to their prescribed roles and the fact they see your loved one on a regular basis, physicians can play a critical role in identifying, treating, and preventing abuse and neglect in institutional settings or in the independent-living environment of the home. When it comes to a group environment, state laws require that patients be admitted by physicians to nursing homes (and, in some cases, to other types of residential facilities). After admission, each resident's care must be under the supervision of an attending physician (or a physician assistant, nurse practitioner, or clinical nurse specialist supervised by a physician), and facilities are mandated to provide them immediate access to their patients.

Several of their prescribed roles make personal physicians more likely to recognize and prevent the institutional abuse and neglect of our loved ones. These roles can include:

- Participating in the development and monitoring of your parent's plan of care
- Assessing the need for and prescribing drugs only when appropriate for treatment of a particular condition, and not for behavioral modification or control
- Monitoring reports that by law must go to the physician, including any irregularities in drug regime as found by the pharmacist who conducts a regular drug regimen review of all patients

Whether a vulnerable elder lives independently or in a home, personal physicians can play a crucial role in the identification and prevention of mistreatment by ongoing monitoring of a patient's health through regular physical exams, review of the patient's record, and review of assessments by others like medical specialists.

Assessments must be completed annually, with updates quarterly and whenever there is a significant change in the patient's condition.

Documentation

Thorough, well-documented medical records are essential. You should help your physician to keep records by taking meticulous notes yourself and maintaining copies of both the doctor's notes and your own. Records should be kept in a precise, professional manner and should include the following:

- Chief complaint and description of the abusive event or neglectful situation, using the patient's own words whenever possible
- Complete medical history
- Relevant social history
- A detailed description of injuries, including type, number, size, location, stages of healing, color, resolution, possible causes, and explanations given
- Where applicable, the location and nature of the injuries should be recorded on a body chart or drawing.
- An opinion on whether the injuries were adequately explained
- Results of all pertinent laboratory and other diagnostic procedures
- Color photographs and imaging studies, if applicable
- If the police are called, the name of the investigating officer and any actions taken

In addition to complete written records, photographs are particularly valuable as evidence. The physician should ask your parent for permission to take photographs. When your parent is unable to give consent, photographs may be taken and a surrogate decision-maker (such as yourself) may need to be consulted after the fact. Imaging studies also may be useful. State laws that apply to the taking of photographs usually apply to X-rays as well.

Legal Considerations

The first priority of the physician when mistreatment is detected or suspected is to assure the safety of the victim. The second is to report the case to the appropriate state agency, such as Adult Protective Services, in accordance with state laws that govern elder abuse and neglect. Your physician's legal obligations may vary depending on whether your parent lives independently, resides at home, or is in an institution. In cases of abuse or neglect in the home, the physician simultaneously may request a variety of other services, including respite care, a visiting nurse service, and a social work evaluation. Awareness of some general principles in the initial stages, such as not confronting the perpetrator and not blaming the victim, is likely to result in a better outcome. The patient's safety and well-being is the goal of any intervention, and must be the physician's primary concern.

A competent older adult who is not being coerced may choose to stay in an abusive situation. In such cases, the physician's role in assessment and referral may be more complicated than it would be for an incompetent patient. On the other hand, most patients and their families welcome physician support and referrals for home services and respite care. This is particularly true when mistreatment results from the caregiver being over-burdened and there is no malicious intent. It is usually less intrusive and threatening to the family to have these interventions suggested by a physician or other professional who is known to them than by an unfamiliar physician or caseworker.

The primary care physician can participate in ongoing management or at least serve as a monitor who can reactivate assistance if the situation is deteriorating and provide follow-up after a referral has been made. If an abused elderly person is treated by a physician who does not inquire about or make an assessment for elder mistreatment, that physician may be held liable for any subsequent injuries. In some states, failure to report is a misdemeanor, the penalty for which may be a fine or even imprisonment.

Elder mistreatment is a complex problem that requires the assistance of a variety of individuals including social workers, visiting nurses, in-home health aides, and occasionally legal and financial experts. Geriatric assessment programs at large hospitals are ideally equipped to respond in these situations. The alternative is for informal community-based teams to respond on an ad hoc basis. A multidisciplinary approach benefits the victim of mistreatment and also lessens the burden of responsibility shared by the professionals involved in the case.

Duty to the Victim

You should know that most physicians will encounter cases of elder abuse and neglect in their practices. They are used to speaking with families about this topic so you should not be reluctant to bring up any concerns you may have. Physicians are aware of their obligations in these cases, as well as their potential liability for failing to diagnose and/or report cases of suspected mistreatment. In general, doing what is medically best or most appropriate is good risk management.

A good physician must be willing to ask all elderly patients about mistreatment and should know how to diagnose it. Failure to conduct the interview and examination apart from the suspected perpetrator may interfere with an accurate diagnosis. Your parent's physician must be ready, willing, and able to intervene in situations that are particularly dangerous for an elderly person: repeated, similar injuries, malnutrition or dehydration, under or overmedication, mental illness in the patient or caregiver; substance abuse by the patient or caregiver; and threatened suicide by the caregiver (there may be increased risk for a murder/suicide).

In states that have enacted mandatory reporting statutes, a physician's failure to report could give rise to liability, but since reporting laws rarely explicitly give victims such a right to sue, courts must determine whether their state's statutes implicitly contain that right. Physicians could be liable, however, under various common law tort actions, including negligence or wrongful death.

Most states provide that reports of suspected mistreatment are kept strictly confidential. Reporters' names may not be released without written consent. In addition, the physician is immune from any civil or criminal liability for making a good faith report of suspected abuse or neglect. To be held liable for reporting, the physician would have to be shown to be acting in a knowingly and intentionally false and malicious manner. Reports made in the context of employment are also generally protected against employer retaliation by "whistleblower" and other public welfare statutes.

Reporters should not be reluctant to report incidents or concerns because they seem "minor" or "not threatening"; physicians should report any reasonable suspicion of abuse or neglect. State reporting agencies will prioritize cases and can provide needed interventions, such as emergency food and care, transportation, medical evaluation, relocation, legal assistance, and other community-based services.

Duty to Warn

Many states recognize a legal duty that physicians have toward third parties who might be harmed by their patients. In those states, if a physician is aware of a patient's intent to harm a third party, such as the patient's spouse or parent, the physician may have a legal duty to breach the patient's confidence and to warn the third party of the impending danger. Physicians, and especially therapists, should know the law where they practice.

The Role of the Attorney

When you hire an attorney, it's your obligation to make sure he or she completely understands the rationale for your estate planning decisions. If you want to matter as a client, you will need to make clear your priorities, your goals, and your rationale for the plans you have in protecting your parents.

You must make sure that your parent fully comprehends the consequences of the decisions he or she is making. You should attend all planning sessions with your parent and any attorney in order to make sure that undue influence is not being exerted against the best interests of your parent or your family. Any good attorney will allow you to record planning sessions so that no details are overlooked and a transcript can be made to preserve your notes regarding the advice being given.

If questions have been raised about your parent's capacity for understanding complex legal matters or the drafting of documents, it will be all the more important to make a proper record of any discussions with lawyers and doctors.

A well-respected attorney named Adam Streisand, who had famously been involved in a case of the questionable competency of Donald Sterling, former owner of the NBA's Los Angeles Clippers, was once the featured speaker before a ballroom full of estate planning professionals at Seattle's Washington Convention Center. He described the basic ethical duties that lawyers have to their clients as follows:

> One basic duty that you have is the **duty to communicate** with your client. You have a duty to keep your client reasonably informed. The client is the one who makes the decisions and you, as the lawyer, need to ensure that you have the informed consent of your client. Now, in order to have informed consent you have to know whether your client understands the decisions that they're making. That means you need to be able to communicate with them.
>
> You have a **duty of loyalty**. And this presents a really fascinating question for estate planning lawyers because lawyers who think about, whether it's loyalty or disloyalty to a client,

when you think the client is slipping, whether you are going to prepare documents, whether you feel a compulsion to tell somebody that the client is slipping, not be able to make rational decisions, are you being loyal or disloyal to the client?

You have a **duty to avoid conflicts of interest**. You have a duty to ensure that you're not taking the position adverse to the client's interest. Are you taking the position adverse to the client's interest when a client tells you that he or she wants to make a change to an estate planning document, and you feel that client doesn't have capacity, and you feel you need to tell somebody? Are you protecting the client's interests or taking a position that's adverse to the client's interest?

You have a **duty of confidentiality**. Now, in California at least, we have business and professions Code 6068, which is far broader than attorney/client privilege and I think most states have similar rules. It isn't just a question of you keeping in confidence legal advice between you and your client. You have a duty to keep in confidence, in strictest confidence, all of your client's secrets, even those having nothing to do with legal advice. And the only exception, at least in California, is to prevent criminal activity that can result in substantial poverty, bodily injury, or death.

And of course, you have a **duty to competence**. And that includes being diligent.

So again, these duties can be at odds with your interest in protecting clients. Can you tell the client's family or a family member if you feel the client is unable to resist undue influence, or maybe lacks capacity? Is it an observation or can you ignore statements the client has made to you that leads you to that sad conclusion? Is that confidence or simply a secret that you were not allowed to divulge?

If you do take action, such as informing somebody that you think a client needs help, that may very well lead to limiting the client's rights. A conservatorship may be established or an adult guardianship. Are you taking a position that's adverse to the client?

Many of us have in our trusts provisions that allow for our removal if we lack capacity. Can you do anything to invoke that provision? Can you tell anybody that the provision even exists? Often what I tell lawyers is try to get something in writing with your client, in advance, that gives you permission under certain circumstances to be able to divulge information to a family member or a trusted advisor if you do have concerns and you think that those provisions ought to be. Certainly a lot of clients aren't going to want to do that. Forty states have adopted ABA model rule 1.14, that does not include California. But that at least gives lawyers implied right to disclose information reasonably necessary to protect a client's interest. You can even consult with individual's amenities with establishing a conservatorship. And many estate planning lawyers believe that that rule makes sense. They know better than anyone what their client would want or when their client needs help.

Traditionally, we have thought that the very low standard testamentary capacity implies the execution of both wills and trusts. And that standard is: does the client have the ability to know who their close relatives are, the ability to know the general nature of their assets, the ability to understand the testamentary act? By the way, "ability" is the word in statute. You don't actually have to know those things, if you can be taught at the moment and retain it at the moment you execute it, you have capacity. This is a low standard capacity.

The question is always going to be: what is the complexity of the decision? This again really emphasizes the need for a lawyer to really engage with his or her client, know why your client is making the decisions they're making, make sure that they really understand the substance of what they're agreeing to so that you can say, I had this relationship with my client. I was a trusted advisor. I know what my client wanted. I know why the client made these decisions, and this is so particularly important when the client suffers from some diminished capacity.

By considering these concerns raised by Mr. Streisand—in matters where ethics and questions of competency intersect—you now have the basis for an opening conversation with any lawyer you may want to hire regarding your vulnerable loved one and their true capacity to make decisions on their own and with your help.

How to Spot a Bad Attorney

While most successful attorneys are morally upright and worthy of the good reputations they have established over time, there are some practicing bad apples as in any profession. Lawyers can be guilty of elder abuse, just like anyone else. Billing practices that seem abusive to the family of an elderly client may rightly be seen as a form of financial abuse. It is truly ironic that the very people you hire to help protect your loved ones may themselves engage in abusive behavior by egregiously overcharging you or your parent or your parent's estate for their services. Check with your state's Bar Association to see if this or any other type of complaint has ever been filed against the attorney or the law firm you are thinking of retaining.

Billing Test

Before you sign a letter of engagement and pay a retainer to a new attorney, ask to see copies of some old billings. Improper billing is a common practice among unethical attorneys that can cost you many thousands of dollars in the course of a legal engagement. Billing statements should accurately describe the lawyer's work and time in sufficient detail to allow critical review and response by an informed and involved client.

Much like a patient is ultimately responsible for managing his or her own health, it's your job to keep a careful watch on billable hour inflation.

According to Litigation Limited, a Los Angeles consulting firm, there are a number of questionable practices a client should be on guard against.

"Block billing" is an accounting technique whereby lawyers aggregate multiple smaller tasks into a single "block" entry, for which a single time value is assigned. A client may be billed for a full hour, rather than seven tenths of an hour, which is the actual amount of time spent on the client's behalf. The client is essentially paying the lawyer a gratuity of three-tenths of an hour. According to the California State Bar, block billing can inflate the total hours billed to the client by 10–30%. For the average senior lawyer, that can translate to more than a quarter million dollars per year in fees for work that never happened.

Another problem that clients aren't often aware of is billable hour "hoarding." When the economy slows down and billable hours are at a premium, work tends to be retained and billed by more expensive senior attorneys. Thus, we find partners doing associate work, associates doing paralegal work, and paralegals doing secretarial work. The problem arises when hourly rates are not discounted to reflect that the senior person is actually doing lower-level work. But senior partners should not bill partner rates for associate-level tasks and lawyers should never bill for paralegal work. As one court eloquently phrased it, "Michelangelo should not charge Sistine Chapel rates for painting a farmer's barn." Thus, clients must not only be concerned with the amount of time spent on particular tasks, but also need to be careful that those tasks are being handled and billed at the appropriate level.

Unethical lawyers also disguise billable hour inflation by using deliberately vague, confusing, or downright meaningless time entries. For instance, when conducting "legal research," it is the lawyer's burden to describe and explain the necessity of such research. Similarly, clients are often billed for a "telephone conference" or "review documents" without any context, so that the client cannot determine whether the work was necessary, efficient, or assigned at the proper level.

Every client should implement outside counsel guidelines that prohibit block billing, vague entries, rounding-up time, and inefficient staffing.

As the adult relative of a vulnerable elderly citizen, you should never hesitate to question and oppose the methods or the madness of those slick professionals who routinely exploit their vaunted social position to ransack the life savings of our parents and grandparents.

Chapter 8

Abusive Guardianships

by Richard W. Black and Dr. Sam J. Sugar

Richard W. Black grew up on a farm in Pennsylvania and graduated in mechanical engineering from West Virginia University. He worked globally as an executive for GE nearly 20 years and a couple other multinational companies. Black left his job as a vice president of a global textile company in February 2015 to devote 100% of his time to elder advocacy and guardianship reform, primarily in Nevada. Those efforts have gained the support of major local media outlets, the attorney general, the county commissioners, district attorney, and the Nevada Supreme Court chief justice. He has built a coalition of over 50 families who have lost over $30 million in the last five years due to guardianship rulings in violation of Nevada Revised Statutes.

Dr. Sam J. Sugar is a medical internist, former chief medical officer at Sunrise Lifestyle Center, and staff physician at Pritikin Longevity Center in Florida. Dr. Sugar founded Americans Against Abusive Probate Guardianship (AAAPG) which has now grown to be a national organization with outposts in over 40 states. With Dr. Sugar's leadership and urging, advocates for probate reform have been trained and are working hard across the country in an attempt to save innocent elderly citizens from the horrors *of professional guardianship. These suggestions are proposed by Americans Against Abusive Probate Guardianship with additional endorsements pursued via ratification by the National Disability Rights Network and the National Silver Hair Congress.*

Background

Adult guardianship has been used by America's local Family and Probate Courts for many years as a tool to "protect the best interests" of an "alleged incapacitated person" (AIP) and to provide authorities and protections for the court-appointed guardian to act on behalf of the third party. Once an AIP is placed into guardianship they are generically referred to as a "ward."

Guardianships throughout most of the twentieth century were predominantly granted to family members and designated or established friends. In the 1980s the United States began to see significant growth of professional guardians, both private and public, to fulfill the requirements of providing individual protections for those alleged to be without qualified family or who hadn't previously designated a guardian.

Guardianships are awarded via petitioning local civil, probate, or family courts. These local courts are all civil in design and as such rule on "the preponderance of evidence." It has been documented in many locales across the country that these courts most often rule in accordance with the best argument. As a result of the enormous latitude granted these courts, due process, rules of evidence, representation, and confirmation that interested parties were notified are often overlooked as they seek to quickly clear their dockets. Predatory lawyers have successfully exploited this environment for their personal benefit.

Routinely, predatory attorneys and the guardians they represent align themselves with guilty parties or against the designated estate party to create a conflict with the intent to deny the estate documents and advanced directives of the victim. Durable powers of attorney, trusts, and wills are commonly denied by this process. Fraudulent claims of criminal activity against the innocent parties are never substantiated due to the reduced burden of proof in a civil court while the desired effect is realized.

Many elder-law attorneys have mastered their ability to fully leverage the lack of due process or requirement of evidence in the family court system to, in essence, criminally prosecute and convict the victim and their innocent family members. Once a temporary guardianship is established, the hyper-accelerated consumption of estate funds begins and the resulting funds flow into the guardian's pockets. The innocent are punished.

Thousands of cases have been reported nationwide where legitimate estate documents and advance directives have been denied by these courts in their haste to appoint professional guardians. Appeals and litigation by designated family members are uniformly ignored by the court in what appears to be biased alignment with established allies of the court.

It has been estimated by the National Center for State Courts and AARP that 1.3 million adults were under guardianship in 2015. It is estimated that 176,000 seniors were placed under guardianship in 2015 and their assets, estimated at $50 billion in total, will be transferred to third parties by local courts.

Concerns with Civil and Disability Rights Protections

Granting guardianship over an AIP removes their civil rights protected under the fourteenth Amendment of the US Constitution. By definition, placing an AIP into guardianship deems them a person with disabilities. Persons with disabilities are protected under Federal law through the Americans with Disabilities Act of 1990.

Most courts nationwide do not have policies in place to insure independent legal representation obligated to protect the best interests of the disabled person being proposed for guardianship. They do not have training programs in place to train and ensure accountability of those attorneys representing those disabled persons being proposed for guardianship.

It has become apparent nationwide that local courts are systematically removing federally protected rights from individuals through guardianship rulings with little consideration for the protections provided by federal law.

Requirements to Serve as a Guardian

There is no uniform federal law or code to defining requirements to serve as a guardian of the estate of a person. Minimum requirements in many states are only that you be 18 years of age. No background checks, no credit checks, no formal education, and no certification or license of a guardian are required in most states. If one has the confidence of the court or a lawyer, almost anyone can serve as a "professional" guardian.

Lack of Oversight

The Government Accountability Office (GAO) conducted an investigation on guardianship abuse and oversight in 2010 at the request of Senator Herb Kohl, chairman of the Senate Special Committee on Aging. Their report highlighted serious issues with abuse in the system and deficiencies in court oversight. Complaints and petitions highlighting wrongdoing by guardians in family court were almost always ignored. Any criminal charges or convictions occurred only when the professional guardian's criminal actions were reported directly to law enforcement by bank officials or private citizens.

CBS News reported in December 2010 that

> A guardian is appointed by the court to "guard" finances and make care decisions for an elderly person who has nobody else to help. Most people think once the court steps in, the person is protected, and safe.
>
> But instead of helping, the guardian drains the person's bank account. What's worse, the court gives its stamp of approval. How could this be happening?

According to GAO investigators, and other investigators from the office of Senator Herb Kohl, "it's the result of unscrupulous actors; piecemeal regulations from state to state; and poor oversight." No federal and very few state reforms have been adopted since Kohl's investigation.

Most states, but not all, require by law that guardians report to the court the initial inventory of their wards and an annual accounting for each of their wards. However, recent studies conducted in Florida, Nevada, California, and Texas, where widespread abuse has been reported, show compliance to state law by local judicial districts ranges from 4 to 30%. The vast majority of guardianships are not compliant with state law.

Often the burden of judicial and legal accountability and oversight falls on the shoulders of legitimate family members or estate heirs, if they exist. In this poorly managed environment, the guilty parties (lawyers and guardians) enjoy carte blanche authority over the ward and their estate. AAAPG estimates that approximately $10 billion per year is converted to third parties through fraudulent guardianships today. That figure is projected to double by 2030 given population projections for those over 65 years of age and projected fraud growth rates.

Summary

The number of fraudulent guardianships and the resulting guardianship abuse continues to rise in America. Local and state courts callously continue to ignore their obligation to protect the civil and disability rights of those presented to them for guardianship protection. Without immediate federal oversight forcing compliance by local courts, the abuse will only continue to rise.

Chapter 9

Pursuing Justice

by Tom Coleman

Thomas F. Coleman is legal director of the Disability and Abuse Project of Spectrum Institute.

The Conservatorship System

I have been fighting oppressive and overbearing economic and legal systems my whole life.

My first experience was with an unfair economic situation in Detroit. A major newspaper was taking advantage of newspaper delivery boys who were under my supervision. I was fired when I tried to organize the boys into a union so they could collectively demand fair working conditions.

Intervention by the National Labor Relations Board resulted in my reinstatement, but I dropped the union organizing because, as a teenager myself, I lacked the resources to press the matter further. To me, that system was rigged. A battle between a group of teenagers and a large corporation had a predetermined outcome. As expected, the system won.

My next encounter with a rigged system came a decade later in California. This time it was with an unfair criminal justice system that sent undercover vice officers to gathering spots for gay men to entrap and arrest them. I was fresh out of law school and started defending these victims of the vice squad.

That system was definitely rigged. The police and the judges knew the men would not fight back. The legal system could count on a plea bargain in almost every case because the deck was stacked against homosexuals even though the crimes involved consenting adults.

The legal profession provided these defendants with a lawyer, but the attorneys counseled their clients that plea bargaining was the only viable option. Few lawyers took cases to trial to contest the charges. None of them challenged the system itself. None, that is, until I took up the cause.

I decided to challenge the constitutionality of the system itself. It took several years of litigation—with plenty of losses along the way—but I finally got a case to the California Supreme Court.

After 18 months of review, the court handed down a landmark decision in *Pryor v. Municipal Court*—a ruling where it declared that the law and the system of enforcement were unconstitutional. It set new rules that all but ended undercover entrapment and the resulting need for defendants to plea bargain.

Fast forward to 2013 when I was confronted with another rigged system. This time it was one that was operated by the probate courts in California. The victims of the rigging were vulnerable adults with intellectual and developmental disabilities and seniors with other cognitive impairments. The legal machine in question was the conservatorship system.

Conservatorship proceedings are initiated, often by parents or relatives, for the protection of seniors or adults with cognitive disabilities who are at risk of neglect because they cannot make major life decisions for themselves. Some states call them guardianship proceedings.

Over the course of 18 months, several cases came my way. The first involved alleged abuse by a conservator of his ward, while another involved numerous rights violations, including the threatened loss of voting rights. In each situation, I was asked to give advice about whether the disabled adult was receiving proper legal representation from a court-appointed lawyer.

My investigation showed a pattern of negligent representation. I began to wonder if these were isolated incidents or if perhaps I was being introduced to another rigged system.

Three years later, after 3,000 hours of analyzing the conservatorship system in California and similar systems in other states, I have concluded that the probate courts are operating a rigged system that is all too often meting out assembly-line injustice to hundreds of thousands of seniors and adults with disabilities.

When a conservatorship petition is filed with the court and served on a senior or an adult with a developmental disability, that person is involuntarily drawn into complicated legal proceedings. Because of cognitive and communication disabilities, there is no way these individuals can question or challenge the petition, much less produce evidence that they should retain some or all of their fundamental rights. The proceedings seek to take away their right to make decisions we all take for granted as adults, involving medical, financial, educational, residential, social, sexual, and marital matters.

"Protective" systems like this exist in all 50 states. There are more than 1.5 million adults in the United States who are currently under an order of guardianship or conservatorship.

In at least 20 states, it is not mandatory for the court to give these adults a lawyer. How rigged is that? Imagine yourself with a cognitive disability, perhaps even unable to speak, and then being served with legal papers in a proceeding that seeks to remove your decision-making rights and confer them on another person. The proposed guardian may even be someone who has been abusing you physically or exploiting you financially.

Then there are 30 states that do give a lawyer to the adult in question. After auditing the system in California and consulting with advocates in other states, I have concluded that the policies and practices in state courts throughout the nation are not giving clients adequate advocacy and defense services.

These state-run probate court systems remain perpetually rigged because of a perfect storm of circumstances. Legislators turn a blind eye to the situation because their primary concern is limiting judicial budgets. Judges must manage huge caseloads and often discourage lawyers from filing motions and demanding hearings simply because these proceedings take up precious court time. Court-appointed lawyers depend on a flow of future cases from the judges who appoint them and so they are afraid to rock the boat. Troublemakers or those who put in "too many hours" on cases fear they may not be appointed to future cases.

Another element of this perfect storm of circumstances perpetuating the status quo is the inability of these litigants to complain. Because of their cognitive and communication disabilities, they do not file appeals with higher courts or lodge complaints with state bar associations. Thus the usual corrective systems are never activated and the pattern of deficient advocacy continues indefinitely.

I have taken up the call of reform. My goal is that litigants with cognitive or communication disabilities will routinely receive individualized justice and due process of law. My hope for a better future rests more with the US Department of Justice (DOJ) than with state officials.

The DOJ could open a formal inquiry into the California policies and practices that violate the Americans with Disabilities Act (ADA)—a federal law requiring courts, and the attorneys they appoint to these cases, to provide access to justice to people with disabilities.

That is not systematically occurring in California now, has not occurred in the past, and is not likely to happen in the future unless and until California is required to answer to a higher authority. The ADA, as administered by the DOJ, is that higher authority.

The DOJ has seen and tackled rigged systems before. Federal intervention now could stimulate conservatorship reform in California, which in turn could launch a domino effect to unrig state guardianship systems throughout the nation.

We Need to Fix Complaint Procedures for Elderly and Disabled Litigants

I sent a letter to the State Bar of California in October 2015 to bring to its attention deficiencies in legal services provided by court-appointed attorneys representing clients with cognitive disabilities in conservatorship proceedings. I sent a similar letter to the California Supreme Court.

For judges and attorneys who interact with litigants who have cognitive disabilities, the ADA—and its mandate that litigants with disabilities are provided access to justice—require that each day must be disability awareness day for the judiciary and the legal profession.

Attorneys who represent clients with cognitive disabilities are bound by the same rules governing attorney-client relationships as are attorneys who represent clients without disabilities. Rules of professional conduct, promulgated by the Supreme Court and enforced by the state bar, require attorneys to perform competently, avoid conflicts of interest, and adhere to ethical duties of undivided loyalty and utmost confidentiality. They must also communicate effectively with their clients. A violation of any of these duties—rooted in common law, statutes, and rules of court—may be addressed through a variety of complaint procedures.

In a criminal proceeding, for example, a disgruntled defendant can ask the court to replace a court-appointed attorney who the defendant feels is performing incompetently. This triggers what is known as a "Marsden" hearing where the defendant can air any grievances in a confidential hearing. A "Marsden" procedure is theoretically available to respondents in conservatorship cases. If the complaint is found to have merit, a new attorney is appointed.

A client who has received ineffective assistance of counsel in a legal proceeding has the right to appeal to bring the complaint to the attention of an appellate court. If the appeal is successful, a new trial may be ordered.

A client who has been victimized by an attorney's misconduct or incompetent services can file a complaint with the state bar. If an investigation shows probable cause that statutes or court rules were violated, an administrative hearing is conducted, which may result in discipline to the attorney. These complaint procedures are theoretically available to all clients, but in reality they are not accessible to litigants with cognitive disabilities. Because of the nature of such disabilities, litigants in conservatorship proceedings, for example, would not know whether their attorneys are performing incompetently, have a conflict of interest, have been disloyal, or have violated the duty of confidentiality. This type of disability also makes them unaware that complaint procedures are available or to understand how to go about filing such a complaint.

Clients with cognitive disabilities are, in a practical sense, unable to make a Marsden motion, file an appeal, or lodge a complaint with the bar association. Unless the judiciary and the legal profession take affirmative measures to provide such clients meaningful access to these complaint procedures, litigants with cognitive disabilities will continue to be excluded from this aspect of the administration of justice.

Solutions are available if only they are sought. There are three public entities in California—each of which has obligations under Title II of the ADA—that should seek solutions so that litigants with cognitive disabilities have access to these attorney complaint procedures.

The Judicial Council of California adopts rules governing trial and appellate court procedures. It should consider a new rule to give "next friend" standing to a third party to make a Marsden motion on behalf of a respondent in a conservatorship proceeding. A more liberal rule on standing should also be adopted to allow a third party to file an appeal when the rights of a litigant with a cognitive disability have been violated due to attorney misconduct or judicial error or abuse of discretion.

The State Bar of California has a major role to play. Knowing that clients with cognitive disabilities will generally not be aware of attorney misconduct or incompetent services, the bar association should allow a third party to initiate a complaint against an attorney suspected of violating rules of professional conduct.

The state bar can also take proactive measures to minimize deficient legal services to litigants with cognitive disabilities. For example, it can monitor training programs for public defenders and court-appointed attorneys who represent respondents in conservatorship proceedings to ensure they are ADA-compliant and that they make the attorneys qualified to handle such cases. Minimum Continuing Legal Education credits should only be allowed for ADA-certified educational programs.

The state bar also can annually audit a sample of conservatorship cases throughout the state to verify, after the fact, that the attorneys truly provided the clients effective advocacy services. Knowing that his or her case might be selected for an audit could have a positive effect on attorney performance.

In addition to its adjudicative role in litigation, the California Supreme Court has an administrative function as well. It is a "public entity" with responsibilities under Title II of the ADA to ensure access to justice for litigants with disabilities. It should exercise its administrative responsibilities by convening, or instructing the state bar to convene, a task force on access to attorney complaint procedures. Such a task force—composed of attorneys, judges, and representatives of organizations advocating for seniors and people with intellectual disabilities—would delve deeper into how to give clients with cognitive disabilities better access to justice if and when their attorneys fail them.

If the state judiciary and the legal profession heed this call to action, the Supreme Court, the state bar, and the judicial council will have found some viable methods of providing meaningful access to these complaint procedures for litigants with intellectual disabilities.

PART 3
FINISHING STRONG

Chapter 10

How to Video Record Your Loved One's Wishes

by Christopher Taylor

Christopher Taylor is primarily known for his directing and cinematography work on top-rated television shows and as a producer, director, and cinematographer on numerous professional projects. Chris began his career as a lighting designer and production stage manager for touring rock acts like the Beach Boys, Bob Dylan, John Fogerty, Simon & Garfunkel, Glenn Frey, and others. Chris currently creates original social-issue programming and his documentaries have won universal praise, including the Audience Award from the International Documentary Association and multiple awards in film festivals world-wide. Chris is an honors graduate of Harvard College and the cinematography program at the American Film Institute.

The old phrase "a picture is worth a thousand words" has no greater relevance than in the landscape of protecting your loved ones from avaricious outsiders. More than a great idea, in our modern age of camera phones and social media it has become a relatively simple act to create a video record as an adjunct to written documentation of your elder relative's preferences when it comes to financial, legal, and health care matters.

You should make this video as early as possible in the chronology of your loved one's late-in-life estate planning. The underlying reason is obvious: a visual record will establish a baseline of mental and physical competence that will empower anyone to verify the authenticity of your elder's wishes going forward.

A clear and accurate video record becomes a unique tool for the future, useful in daily life as well as inside a courtroom. No written documents with signatures can irrefutably establish competency in such a powerful way. In fact, some lawyers who have built substantial practices by winning cases against family members (in favor of private guardians, for instance), frequently counsel their clients to "avoid videotaping" because it can provide valuable evidence as well as memories of sentimental value to the elderly and their families.

I am also strongly recommending that you do not wait until an emergency has arisen to make this record, as the resulting video should reveal a natural ease and comfortable stress-free relationship between all parties involved in the process.

The first step in creating a video record to memorialize your loved one's wishes is to select a camera. You can use your iPhone (or similarly-equipped smartphone or tablet), but I am going to recommend that you use a dedicated stand-alone camera.

First, you will want to be able to control some of the parameters of recording—especially sound—in a way that is difficult (or impossible) with a camera app/smartphone. A dedicated camera keeps the quality of your recording reasonably high and in focus. Be sure to use a tripod for steadiness. If the digital video recording is ever exhibited before a group in a legal or judicial setting, it's very likely that the resolution and overall image quality will be diminished by whatever projection system is employed. Therefore, you will want to begin with the highest quality image that your camera can produce.

Nowadays, HD cameras with native resolutions of 1920x1080p are available for a few hundred dollars. This will suffice. (At the point of this writing, you don't need to worry about the latest technology like UltraHD or 4K. That may change in a few years, but for right now save yourself the expense of these broadcast quality formats.)

Here are some useful tips for shooting:

1. As mentioned, *use a tripod whenever possible.* This will guarantee image steadiness and help to maintain consistent focus.

2. *Engage all auto functions* (Focus, Exposure, and White Balance) on your camera. Check in the camera's LCD or viewfinder that you can plainly and clearly see the facial details of anyone who speaks on camera. All faces should be clearly exposed and in focus. When someone is saying something important, he or she should be framed in a close-up so that their face fills the frame.

3. Do not put your subject in front of a window, as this will drive the autoexposure to close down. If there's a choice, film a subject where the window provides sidelight or front light. Try to shoot your loved one in the daytime. Usually the energy level of those involved is better and the overall light level will help make everything look better. If you have to shoot at night, turn all available lights on but try not to have artificial bright lights anywhere inside the frame.

4. You should have a few friends and/or family members present at the scene to act as witnesses, and it's a good idea for everyone to identify themselves on camera. If you have witnesses in the room, they should be people that you can reach out to and who will be

willing to show up at a legal hearing or courtroom to support the record you are making. (This is also a reason why it's not good to rely on health-care workers or others not known to you as you may have difficulty tracking them down at some point in the future.)

5. *Get a good shotgun mic* (like a Rode VideoMic Pro) that mounts to the top of your camera. This is very important and is often over-looked, but the quality of the sound and the ability to clearly hear and understand the spoken wishes of loved ones—who may speak softly or in a halting manner—will often make the difference in being able to create a binding legal record. Also, make sure that distracting sounds are not present. This could be a TV or music, unsupervised children, unrelated conversations, or the like. It is important to make sure that the room is quiet, there are no com-peting sounds, and that your loved one can be heard clearly and distinctly. As you are recording, you should listen to the audio over headphones or earbuds plugged into the camera's audio-out jack to make sure that the audio signal is clear and free of noise, hiss, rumble, and other distractions. If you have any questions or doubts about how to get the right microphone, take your camera to your local A/V store and show them the various inputs and outputs and ask for the right shotgun mic to get your job done correctly. You can also call one of the major online retailers and explain what you want/need, and one of their customer service reps will recommend the right microphone or other piece of equipment. Expect to pay around $200–$300 for a good quality shotgun microphone.

6. More about sound: in the camera LCD (or viewfinder) there should be an audio meter display showing the level of the incom-ing audio. To be safe you should not be seeing constant "red" in the audio level meter. This indicates that the audio is distorting (and you should be hearing this distortion on your headphones). The

ideal level for sound in conversation is usually measured around -8 to -12 dB, and there should be numbers on the audio meter that reflect this. If there are no numbers, make sure that your audio meter shows signal in the green area but not red. Occasional peaks that go into red are tolerable, but constant red is not. Technical details aside, you can also rely on the sound you hear in your head-set—if it's good quality, then you should be fine.

7. When you record your loved one, start with a wide shot that shows the room and those present. Then zoom into a medium close up of your loved one and ask them to please state their name and the date, and then to declare his or her motivation for making the tape recording.

8. Your subject may then read from their "last will and testament." The statement should be direct and to the point and usually shorter is better, but make sure to cover every area that you are concerned about. In general it's good to get these statements in "one take" and without distracting camera movements.

9. After this statement you should also get name information from each witness.

10. Before you end your efforts, make sure to watch (and listen) to the video you have made. Once you are sure that you have recorded what you need, you can pack everything up.

One last suggestion for filming: if you are in a hurry and do not have access to any of the above (camera, tripod, etc.) of course, you can simply use your iPhone or a similar phone camera. Since I know the iPhone platform I will make recommendations for software that works for it. In most cases the same software exists for other platforms.

- You should do this right now: on your phone go to Settings>
  Photos & Camera>Camera>Record Video and select 1080p at
  30 FPS. FYI you can select 1080p at 60 FPS, but that will
  make the files larger and a little more difficult to move around.
- If you feel comfortable with photography, download the app
  "Filmic Pro" and set it up for 30 FPS and set audio to iPhone
  Microphone Back, AIFF, 48.0 kHz.
- Check your recordings immediately after you make them.

The advantage of FilmicPro is that it shows you the audio level, which
should give you confidence that you are recording sound properly.

One challenge with using your phone is that it takes a little extra
effort to get the video files off your phone so that you can distribute
copies and archive them for storage. If you have files that are more than
two minutes in running time (or are too large to e-mail), you can use
several techniques to get them off your phone and onto your computer.
On a Mac you can use iPhoto or Image Capture to download them
(or the apps iFunbox or Copytrans) and once they are on your computer you can use a file sharing service like Dropbox to allow others to
download them. It is very important that you distribute the video files
to your family lawyer or any representative that will be part of your
family's legal team. You should also send the files to interested family
members so that they are up to date on your loved one's wishes. And
you should make several copies on different hard drives for archival
safety. I cannot stress strongly enough that you need to have multiple
archival copies.

At the end of the day, videotaping your loved one as early as possible
is important for one other reason. If it should happen that an opportu-
nistic caregiver or guardian attempts to change any of the parameters
(power of attorney, health care decisions, estate planning issues, etc.)
when your loved one is no longer competent, your original video will
provide a basis for judgment in this area that will enforce your loved

one's true intentions. They say "the camera never blinks," and this fact is hugely important for you and your family.

Chapter 11

Telling the Story

by David Steen Martin

David Steen Martin is a former senior investigative producer with Al Jazeera America and executive producer with CNN, where he made documentaries with Chief Medical Correspondent Dr. Sanjay Gupta. Martin has received Gold Medals at the New York Television and Film Festival for the documentary CNN Presents: By Penalty of Death *and for Best Investigative Report for* CNN Presents: Soldier Guinea Pigs. *He was nominated for an Emmy for Best Documentary Research on CNN's* Toxic Towns USA *and has received two National Headliner Awards for his work. Martin also wrote and directed the feature-length documentary* Fully Charged. *He holds a master's degree in journalism from Columbia University and has reported extensively both nationally and internationally. He lives in Lincoln, Nebraska, with his wife and three children.*

Oscar Olivera (not his real name) was a larger-than-life figure in Santa Fe. An accountant by training, the bearded Olivera liked pickup trucks and painting, and had taken up acting in middle age, landing roles in major motion pictures with Hollywood stars. Family members joked Bob had swag before anyone knew what swag was. When the 68-year-old fell and broke a kneecap in 2012, requiring rehab, his daughter picked a nursing home nearby so she could make daily visits. Olivera didn't need surgery, but the big man needed physical therapy to strengthen his left knee before he could go home.

"I was naïve enough to think if I was there every day that nothing would happen to my dad," his daughter recalled. Olivera's family expected him to return to his home within the month, but just two weeks after checking into a local nursing home his daughter received a telephone call saying her father had a low-grade fever and was being taken to the local emergency room. The nursing home downplayed the trip to the hospital, saying it was merely a precaution, but Olivera's condition was serious. At the hospital, a nurse told Olivera he had a stage IV pressure ulcer that had penetrated through skin to muscle. Worse still, the bedsore had become infected and required surgery. The next day, following an operation, Olivera's surgeon delivered more bad news. Olivera's infection had spread to his bloodstream. He never recovered. The coming months were a downward spiral for Olivera: three more operations, a tracheotomy, intubation, feeding tube, colostomy bag, dialysis, ventilator. Olivera turned 69 in an acute care facility 60 miles from home, in Albuquerque.

"We were given the talk by the doctor that 'your father is never coming off the machines,'" his daughter recalled. During one of her father's good days, Olivera told his children they had his permission to let him go. He died surrounded by adoring family members.

Olivera's death left his daughter with sadness and a mix of anger and guilt, a potent stew of emotions that brought tears to her eyes more than two years later: How could she have better protected her father? After all, she saw him every day and there were no obvious signs of poor treatment until he was transported to the hospital. She'd even checked out the nursing home before her father arrived. The staff had been welcoming, the facility appeared well run. Also, unlike many nursing home residents, Olivera was lucid, his mind sharp. He could have reported problems directly to his daughter during her visits. Still, the thought tugged at her: What had she missed? What could she have done to prevent the tragedy?

"I will never be over it," Olivera's daughter said last year, shaking her head. "My family will never be over it. I will live with the guilt of my father ever having gone into that place."

The details of Olivera's agonizing final months did not become public until he died, and the family sued. I never met Olivera. I wish I had. I learned about him from his daughter after finding his name in a search of Santa Fe County court records and seeing the caption for the lawsuit against the nursing home. As a producer for a nationally televised news magazine show, I normally would not have been interested in what happened in a at a Santa Fe nursing home, no matter how tragic, but I had been doing research into whether nursing home chains were putting profits ahead of patients when and New Mexico Attorney General Hector Balderas took had taken the unusual step of filing a lawsuit against seven nursing homes and their corporate owners alleging just that.

The state's lawsuit claimed the facilities billed for a level of care that was not provided because staffing levels were dangerously low. One of the nursing homes named in the lawsuit was the nursing home where Olivera went for rehab. According to the attorney general's lawsuit, the inadequate staffing levels at the nursing homes owned by the same parent company resulted in residents being left in soiled clothing or beds, often for hours at a time; suffering unnecessary falls because their call lights went unanswered; losing weight because not enough nursing assistants were on duty to help them eat; developing terrible pressure ulcers because there were not enough staff members to reposition them. As a journalist, I wanted to talk to the people allegedly harmed because of inadequate care at these nursing homes or, as the next best thing, their family members. But New Mexico's lawsuit did not name any of the victims or witnesses to the poor treatment. That led me to public records looking for families with first-hand experience at these nursing homes, and that's where I found Olivera's daughter, who was gracious enough to talk about her family's nightmarish experience.

Even with the horrific claims in New Mexico's lawsuit, none of the local news stations picked up the story. Journalists in general do not spend much time reporting on issues affecting the elderly. Most lack the personal interest and the expertise. Unless they are part of a special investigative team, reporters at local news stations have very little time for any kind of reporting, let alone on a subject that does not interest them, which means they will shy away from complex stories. Also, news organizations want their content to appeal to a younger demographic. The demographic TV executives most care about (because advertisers care about it) is the 25–54 age group. There is a perception (I would say a misperception) that younger people do not want to hear about the elderly. This assumption ignores an important fact: Many in the coveted 25–54 demographic have elderly parents. They are often wrestling with issues about how best to care for their mothers and fathers. The lack of media coverage on the elderly abdicates one of the key responsibilities of journalism: informing readers and viewers, serving as watchdogs. If a restaurant were cooking food in unsanitary conditions, or a supermarket were selling tainted produce, we would expect the news to report it. Yet when inspectors find nursing homes providing substandard care, their findings usually receive no media coverage. Some 1.3 million Americans receive care in nursing homes every day, more than the number of people in the United States infected with HIV, yet they live their lives in the shadows, largely out of view and off the radar screen of news organizations.

Local news usually only reports on elder abuse after someone has died. Most often, the story recounts the horrible allegations, adds comments from grieving and angry family members, and closes with a denial or bland comment from the facility where the alleged abuse took place. The tragedy receives the same sort of lurid and shallow coverage as a random, fatal robbery at an ATM or a small plane crash and then it's time for sports or the weather. What is skipped in this sort of coverage is how the tragedy fits into the bigger picture. Context is everything. Elder abuse does not happen in a vacuum, and it's usually not the result of a lone sociopath. As the lawsuit in New Mexico alleges, something as seemingly benign as staffing levels can have profound effects on the level of care.

This is not to say journalists will never help. They can be a valuable ally, especially when the issue is government accountability. For example, say state inspectors either don't follow up on complaints or routinely conclude that complaints are unfounded. In cases like these, public exposure can embarrass government into doing the right thing. To increase the likelihood your story will be picked up by the media, gather as much evidence as possible. What documents, photographs and video can bolster your claims? If you don't have them yet, gather them in advance of pitching a journalist on your story. Better still, find others who have shared the same experience who are willing to speak out. Most journalists are very busy and they don't have a lot of time to determine if your claims are credible.

Make it as easy as possible for them. Also, when speaking to reporters and producers, keep your anger in check and don't make any claims that you can't back up, no matter how strong your suspicions. This goes back to your credibility. You don't want to appear unhinged or like a conspiracy theorist. Remember, too, you need to explain your situation methodically and simply. You may have been immersed, angered, and frustrated for months or years, but it is all new for the journalist sitting in front of you. A correspondent for whom I have a great deal of respect would call me before we'd head out on a story and ask: How would you describe this story in one or two sentences? It's something you should ask yourself. The exercise will help focus the narrative you share and, again, increase your odds of getting your story in print or on television.

In the absence of the media, family members themselves need to become investigative reporters. I've talked to ordinary folks who have done incredibly diligent digging on very complex subjects. They do the kind of information gathering that is a journalist's stock in trade: scouring the Internet, talking to people, examining public records, filing Freedom of Information Act requests. What follows are my recommendations for how to go about gathering the information you need to minimize the chances of placing a loved one in a nursing home providing shoddy or dangerous care.

The first place to look is Medicare's Nursing Home Compare site (medicare.gov/nursinghomecompare). Medicare uses a star rating system for nursing homes. Five stars is the best. One star is the worst. The star rating is far from perfect but gives a good sense of the overall quality of care. The website offers a lot more valuable information about ownership, staffing, inspections, and care. Family members should check the staffing levels, especially the number of RNs on duty, compared to other nursing homes in the state. As one researcher at the University of California, San Francisco, told me, "RNs are the most important part of the nursing home staffing because they're the ones that can assess the residents. They provide the treatments. They do the planning and the care management, so if you don't have enough of them you're going to have all kinds of quality problems."

Check the percentage of long-term residents who receive antipsychotic medications. Some nursing homes, especially those that are short staffed, use antipsychotics as a way to zonk out their residents and reduce their staffing needs. If you walk into a nursing home where the central hallway is filled with the wheelchairs of sleeping residents, mouths agape, there's a good chance antipsychotics are being used in excess. Nursing homes too often turn to these powerful medications even though the Food and Drug Administration has a black box warning—the agency's most serious—against prescribing antipsychotics for people with dementia because they can cause sudden death. Almost a third of nursing home residents with dementia still receive antipsychotics, despite the government warnings.

Families should also check the Nursing Home Compare's penalties section to see if the facility has paid any fines in the previous three years. Look at the health inspection reports, both the standard health inspections and the complaint inspections. How many mistreatment deficiencies did inspectors find? How many health deficiencies? How serious were the complaints? How does that compare to other nursing homes in the state and nationally? State health departments often put their own inspections and other information online, although sometimes it's difficult to find.

As an investigative producer, I've talked to passionate advocates who have spent their professional lives working to make sure nursing homes do better by seniors. They have some very specific, common-sense advice on how families can avoid placing their loved ones in bad nursing homes. For example, when you walk into a nursing home, does it smell of urine or feces? The smell alone is a telltale sign of understaffing, a tip off that residents' most basic needs are not being met in a timely fashion.

Tony Chicotel, an attorney with the California Advocates for Nursing Home Reform, recommends visiting on nights and weekends. He says you want to see a nursing home when it's at its worst and staffing is at its lowest. Carole Herman, founder of the Foundation Aiding the Elderly, says family members should see if residents have water to drink. "Dehydration is a very serious problem," she said. Tracy Murrell, a former state inspector in New Mexico, says visitors should note whether residents' hair is well groomed and they are dressed nicely. If men are unshaven or women's hair unkempt, or if they are dressed in sweatpants or other clothing that's convenient for the staff, that's a warning sign, Murrell says.

Nursing homes do not like scrutiny. As journalists, we are almost never invited into nursing homes. Usually, we are confronted when we get video of a nursing home's exterior, about the only thing left to shoot if you aren't allowed inside. One afternoon last spring, I stood with my director of photography across the street from a nursing home in Tallahassee, shooting exteriors, when staffers came out to confront us. They first told us to stop shooting. When we told them we were on public property, they demanded to know why we were there. We said we were reporting on a federal inspection report that found the director of nursing at the facility had withheld glucose monitoring strips for 60 residents for more than a month because she thought staffers were wasting them. The inspectors concluded the residents were placed in "immediate jeopardy" by this failure. Still, staffers were indignant that we were there. Driving back to our hotel, a police cruiser pulled us over. The officers told us there had been a report we'd trespassed. It wasn't until we'd shown them our video—taken from across the street—the officers let us go. The next day, I received a call from a woman with a public relations company hired by the nursing homes' corporate owner suggesting we clear any future shoots with them first. Needless to say, I declined.

Nursing homes are big business. More than two-thirds of the 15,600 nursing homes nationally are part of for-profit chains. They want to preserve their reputations—and their profit margins. More than 60% of nursing home reimbursements are paid for by the government, and nursing homes receive the virtually the same federal reimbursement if the care is good or poor. Research by Harrington, the UCSF researcher, has documented methods for-profit nursing homes use to maximize profits, often at the expense of residents. A Kaiser Family Foundation study found for-profit nursing homes were twice as likely to receive one or two stars from Medicare as non-profits.

Even though Olivera's daughter didn't have any obvious signs her father was being mistreated, she did have clues the nursing home had problems right from the beginning. For starters, she said, the air conditioner in Olivera's room didn't function properly when he arrived. This was August in Santa Fe, and his room was muggy as a result. The nursing home also did not initially have his diabetes or pain medications. Olivera also didn't get bathed until his daughter demanded a bath for her father three days into his stay. Around that time, his daughter also realized the inflatable bed designed to prevent pressure ulcers in his first room didn't work, meaning he had to be moved to another room. In the new room, his roommate suffered from dementia and kept Olivera up all night. He was moved again, but during the move, staff left him in a wheelchair for three hours while they waited for a new bed to arrive from Albuquerque. All this prompted Olivera's daughter to decide to take her father out of the nursing home. When his daughter told the nursing home staff she was going to find another rehab facility, the general manager arrived within minutes and said she would personally make sure Olivera had his medications and was otherwise cared for. She agreed to keep him there.

In retrospect, all these small issues loom large. They are a cautionary tale for others with loved ones in nursing homes. The little things can be signs of bigger problems. Olivera had checked in to the nursing home for physical therapy, but even that was problematic. A custom brace needed for his therapy didn't arrive for almost two weeks, meaning Olivera had only two days of physical therapy by the time he went to the hospital with a pressure ulcer.

Olivera's family settled their lawsuit for an undisclosed sum, but money is a small consolation. Memories of the series of events that led to her father's death remain so painful his daughter avoids taking the street where the nursing home is located. Still, she is willing to talk about his case, even if it means dredging up painful memories, hoping her father's story will help others.

"If my father was sitting here in front of me today, the first thing he would say, 'You make sure that this doesn't happen to anyone. You use my story.' It's hard to go through these memories," Olivera's daughter said. If one family could be helped, she said the pain of reliving her father's final months would be worth it.

Chapter 12

Advice for Caretakers

by Dwayne Clark

Dwayne Clark is the founder and chief executive officer of Áegis Living. With more than 28 years of senior housing experience, he has been involved in the development, construction, and/or management of over 200 senior housing projects. He studied business models from companies known for world-class innovation and customer service, such as Costco, Starbucks, Disney, and Four Seasons. He is never satisfied with the traditional care offered by most senior housing companies, but rather relentlessly pursues treatments and global therapies, both Eastern and Western, to bring the best care and a holistic approach for residents' minds, bodies, and spirits. Dwayne's drive for excellence in senior care is personal. His mother became a resident at one of his communities in the advanced stages of Alzheimer's. Dwayne understands the cruelty of this disease and has applied his personal experiences and passion to Áegis Living's highly successful memory care programs.

Intellectually, we know that aging is part of life, but Alzheimer's is a disease that can challenge—and even break—the closest friends and family of someone who suffers from it. If anyone should have been prepared for my mother's disease, it should have been me. I've spent almost my entire professional life devoted to services and communities that care for the elderly, and I've seen all of the difficulties and challenges that patients and their families contend with. But I wasn't prepared—not by a long shot. And throughout my mother's ordeal, I came to the realization that no one ever is.

Intellectually, we know that getting older, getting sick or frail, getting dementia, or even getting Alzheimer's is a part of life. It's not until someone we love—someone we care for and are responsible for—is gradually pulled away from us by the disease that the reality sinks into our hearts and souls. It is natural—and very normal—for family members of a person experiencing dementia and Alzheimer's symptoms to deny that possibility for as long as possible and to attempt to maintain the ordinariness of "regular" life. Yet facing this disease and getting through and beyond denial provides huge benefits for everyone—better medical care leading to better quality of life for the patient and family members, better care-taking of the patient and support for loved ones, and better insight to ease the challenges and create more opportunities for closeness and closure.

When I look back at my story and the journey I've been on as a son and as a professional, I tried to think about what would be most helpful to others. What practical lessons and advice could I share that would make a difference? To-do lists aren't what most of us need. We need to-be lists, to-allow lists, to-know lists, to-accept lists. That's what will help us Alzheimer's families get through as best as we possibly can.

As I thought about what was most helpful to me and what makes the biggest difference with families at Aegis, I realized that understanding is the most powerful thing. When we truly understand what's happening and what will help, it makes our personal choices and decisions much easier. Understanding comes over time, through bits of wisdom, practical medical insights, health strategies, emotional preparations, and support mechanisms that can improve things as much as possible and give us comfort along the way. So what I've come up with are **Fourteen Guidelines for the Journey**, a series of stepping stones to help you find your way. This list may not be all-inclusive for everyone dealing with Alzheimer's, but it helped me and my family as we sought to cope, understand, and find meaning and acceptance—and it had a positive impact on my mother's care and well-being.

Before I present the guidelines, I want to share the gift of the most memorable pieces of advice I received while my mom was sick. These are words and messages from doctors, caregivers, and other family members that I returned to over and over at times when the disease became harder to bear. This is advice that I've since since shared with many others along the way. Highlight the ones that resonate with you and tape them above your desk or dresser or tuck a copy into your wallet so you can read them when you most need to.

- Understand from the outset that things will not improve.
- Ask for and accept help.
- Try to be easy on yourself. This may well be the most difficult thing you'll ever do.
- Try not to feel guilty. None of this is your fault.
- Fill your heart and mind with good things.
- Sometimes, with the afflicted person, comfort is the only victory.
- Remember that you're not supposed to get everything right.
- This time will pass and you will have the memory of how you responded to the challenge.
- When it's time, put away your grief or anger or disappointments and live your life. That's what your parent, grandparent, or spouse would have wanted.
- Take time for yourself to meditate, to walk alone, to sit in silence, and to breathe—and breathe deeply.

- Love all, trust few, always paddle your own canoe.

This last bit of advice is what my mother always used to say. As her son, it's my job to carry that message forward. Now, though, I think she'd appreciate this added sentiment: But even though we are all paddling our own canoe, we all share the same vast ocean of water, trying to make the most of what we are given, trying to find our own truth.

Fourteen Guidelines for the Journey

1. Information Is Healing

We get information in all kinds of ways, and they all support our ability to make sense of the challenges in our lives and in the decisions we face. We get information through:

- real-life stories (like this book) and conversations with friends
- experience as we live, deal with events, and shift in our thinking, feeling, and actual physical responses to a situation
- researching books, articles, websites, lectures, and classes
- intuition, spiritual sources, and the unconscious mind

There are numerous books, videos, organizations, and support groups available and consulting a variety of sources can be particularly clarifying and empowering for anyone coping with Alzheimer's. As such, family members and caregivers should actively seek a deep level of knowledge and understanding as early on as possible—and update that research over time.

This will help you (and other family members) fully grasp the mental and physical implications for the victim of this disease, but it will also help you realize the journey that you have embarked on as well. You will have the tools and knowledge you need to recognize what will be a new kind of normal: the agitation, the paranoia, the phobias, the memory loss. You will understand that your loved one now has memory gaps and will feel and display frustration, even rage, when they can't verbalize their thoughts or recall faces and memories. The person wants to hold onto their identity, and the communication and processing skills necessary to do so, but the disease is getting worse.

As a caregiver, you will feel like perhaps you are losing your own mind too, "going crazy." That's why knowledge of what to expect early on is so critical; knowing what is normal at different stages and what to expect in the future will help assuage any feelings of guilt that may surface and provide much-needed emotional comfort and assurance as you move forward.

2. Use a Physician Specializing in Aging—and Find the Best.

Many older people have had the same internist or general practitioner for twenty or thirty years. They've developed trust in and familiarity with that person and commonly resist turning over their care to someone new—a veritable stranger by their standards. Yet geriatricians, neurologists with a specialty in memory loss, and other doctors with specialties in aging can provide a much higher level of care. They understand the many forms and diagnoses of memory loss, including Alzheimer's disease and Parkinson's, the challenges of nutrition, and the range of treatments and protocols needed to deal with the loss of abilities such as speech and swallowing. Finding the right physician can extend your loved one's life by two to five years—and improve the quality of their life.

There are challenges to finding a qualified physician. To begin with, there is a shortage of geriatricians, and some of these limit the number of Medicaid patients they accept into their practice. Ask for referrals through organizations and your health insurance provider. Consider "best doctor" listings provided by trusted journalistic sources that you can search for on the Internet. Depending on your access to specialists in your community, consider an initial consultation for a treatment plan with preferred physicians. Even if they are based farther away, he or she can at least act as a specialized consultant to your local doctor. When is the right time to make the transition? It's rarely "too soon." When you begin having questions about your loved one's health, care, and memory, that is usually the best indication that the time has come to seek out the expertise of a physician trained in elder medicine.

3. Understand the Disease

Many people "know" something is wrong for months and even years before they seek—and get—an official diagnosis of Alzheimer's disease. In truth, Alzheimer's is a diagnosis of symptoms, as there is no definitive test that documents the disease. A diagnosis can be avoided, delayed, or missed altogether for a number of reasons. Many of the signs of the disease run parallel to the natural aging process, including memory loss, struggle for words, forgetfulness, and perhaps new anxieties, confusion, or neediness. Also, there doesn't seem to be any "good" that comes from the diagnosis, though there can be treatments that substantially slow the disease process. While it is natural for us as human beings to forget things as we age—our brain cells actually begin deteriorating in our early twenties and we all forget where we left our car keys from time to time—it is the repetitive and continued loss of familiar things that should concern us, especially when it interferes with our daily schedule, plans, and relationships.

In the beginning, when we start to see our loved one "getting older" or "declining," it's hard, even impossible, to know if they're experiencing normal aging, an illness that can be treated, or a degenerative disease that can be improved with certain types of care. Our resistance and fears, coupled with the older person's desire to see themselves as "just fine," can keep us from taking actions that will be beneficial and helpful for everyone—and can lead to a much higher quality life. Weight loss, poor nutrition (especially in earlier stages), and depression are coexisting diagnoses, all of which can be managed and even overcome.

Understanding brain function and Alzheimer's

Our brains are superconductors of information. Every second, billions of neurotransmissions, tiny electrical impulses containing messages, travel from one brain cell to another. Electrical and chemical neurotransmitters allow these messages to travel across tiny gaps between the neurons. Alzheimer's causes the network to break down by inhibiting the brain's production of acetylcholine, a chemical that essentially lubricates the brain at the microscopic level. Without this lubricant, a sticky plaque forms and limits the flow of information. In addition, protein fibers within the neurons become twisted and tangled, further diminishing the ability of brain cells to communicate with each other. As a result, memories are lost, behavior changes, and the personality that you associate with the individual eventually disappears.

Although many people lump all memory loss under the umbrella of Alzheimer's disease, there are many different types of memory loss diseases. Huntington's disease, for example, is an inherited brain disorder that destroys brain cells and affects a person's cognitive and physical abilities, but doesn't show until a sufferer is in their thirties and early forties. Parkinson's disease, though sometimes confused with Alzheimer's, is a degenerative disorder of the central nervous system that impairs the muscles. Dementia, from the Latin *de* (without) and *mentia* (mind), a term first used to describe Roman soldiers who had sustained head injuries on the battlefield, is another loss of cognitive brain function that is often associated with Alzheimer's, though it can result from other diseases as well. Dementia symptoms in those suffering from Alzheimer's can manifest differently from person to person. The most prevalent, though, include mood changes, loss of problem-solving skills, difficulty communicating, disorientation, change in personality, and the appearance of new behaviors.

The Seven Stages of the Reisberg Scale

In 1982, Dr. Barry Reisberg published a seven-stage scale of Alzheimer's disease that is used to this day to help assess the disease's progression in individuals. Stage 1 is no impairment. Stage 2 is typical of normal aging and the "senior" moments so many middle-aged people experience. Stages 3, 4, and 5 show progressive impairments in a person's ability to remember, plan, organize, and take care of themselves, with slow declines sometimes followed by precipitous and shocking drops in functioning over the course of days or weeks. The person may start something like cooking a meal and never finish it, or they may have trouble keeping track of their household. Memory aids like notes and reminders may help. There are many ways the disease presents itself as it becomes manifest in this middle period of the disease. Stereotypes are just that—they may or may not reflect any individual's symptoms. Stages 6 and 7 refer to the late stages of the disease where the person is literally disappearing mentally and needs intensive and, ultimately, complete physical care.

General Signs

Some of the more obvious signs of Alzheimer's are difficulty finding the right words. Forgetting that a loved one has passed away and speaking of them as if they are still alive may be common. Short-term memory is quickly affected. You may ask them what they had for lunch the day before and they may not be able to tell you. A person may show changes in behavior and personality, becoming belligerent, loud, flamboyant, or uncooperative. It may feel as if they are just letting their true personality out, or they may be uncharacteristically aggressive, paranoid, or compulsive. Their brain has a drive to fill in information—even if it's made up. The person's self-protective psychology pushes them to cover up.

A Red Flag: The Transient Ischemic Attack (TIA)

A TIA, sometimes referred to as a mini-stroke, can be a red flag for declining health and the risk of developing Alzheimer's. These so-called "warning strokes" produce stroke-like symptoms such as sudden confusion, dizziness, loss of balance, or numbness of the face, arm, or leg. TIAs occur when a blood clot temporarily clogs an artery and part of the brain doesn't get the blood it needs. Most TIAs last less than five minutes and do not cause permanent injury to the brain. To some people, TIAs can seem so minor that they do not get medical treatment afterward, but they are extremely important indicators or predictors of a major stroke or Alzheimer's, and potential clues to other brain or arterial changes that should be evaluated by specialists.

Other coexisting signs

Alcohol use and excessive drinking can co-occur with Alzheimer's and be a way for a person to cover up and ease their anxieties, although it can also be a cause of weaker cognitive function. This complex and hard-to-address scenario should be discussed with the professionals you're working with. Depression and other symptoms and medical conditions should be definitively evaluated and treated to enhance quality of life and as clues for diagnosis. There can be many complications due to multiple medications, side effects, and co-occurring conditions that can affect the health of an older person, but are easy to overlook or not recognize.

4. Watch, Observe, and Journal

Behavior analysis is the only way to diagnose Alzheimer's and to plan the best care and environment to support a person once they've been diagnosed. Family members play a crucial role here and keeping a journal of symptoms and changes can be enormously helpful—I know that it was for me. As soon as you start noticing changes in condition, jot down the dates, what happened, and what's out of the ordinary. It could be eating, breathing, weight gain or loss, or behavior changes such as hiding things or displaying inappropriate anger.

These notes will provide data for a person's decline or improvement. For example, my mother was originally diagnosed with Alzheimer's and later her Parkinson's was identified. When we put her on Parkinson's medication, for about six months she actually improved. She gained weight, she started walking and talking, and the Parkinson's "mask" went away. We wouldn't have had that detailed knowledge if we hadn't written observations down. Remarks like "her face got frozen," on a particular date were helpful for physicians to create treatment plans.

A journal also helps give you a marker of where a person is in the progression of Alzheimer's disease. When a person stops talking or eating, you can see where that falls on the Reisberg scale. The average life span after a person is diagnosed with Alzheimer's is seven years. When my mother reached the final stage at the age of eighty-seven, we knew she was very near the end of her life, and we were able to mark occasions and involve our extended family and friends in a way that felt healing and meaningful for all of us.

5. Look for Love and Understanding When Choosing a Care Facility

I know when I meet new friends and the topic of my business comes up, the response is usually, "My mom would never live in a place like that."

This is when I ask, "Like what?" It seems like most people's impression of assisted living facilities hasn't changed from the stereotype: the sterile, smelly place where people wander around aimlessly and yell in the hallways. When I show them photos of our Aegis communities, the response is always the same: "Wow, I never knew that places like this existed."

There are many options like Aegis today—places of warmth, caring, and professionalism. Once a family or person with memory loss raises the question of needing help or starts discussing a change in living arrangements, that is the best time to take steps to find more care from an assisted living community. No one ever says, "I did this too soon." The emotions are wrenching, but once the initial decision is made, there are straightforward steps and options to consider, and the process usually goes very quickly and with less struggle than the months that preceded it.

If there's been a crisis that precipitates the transition to assisted living, you will find very supportive help and information through the Alzheimer's Association and many agencies in your area. When that moment arrives, how do you choose? How do you imagine what's right, when nothing seems right about the situation at all? There are five factors to consider:

- Type and size of the community and level of care
- Location
- Reputation
- Costs
- And most of all, love and understanding

What is the connection between staff and residents and your sense of their understanding and caring? Every state has different licensing terms and regulations and there are some thirty to fifty licensing categories across the United States, but basically there are four tiers of communities: mom-and-pop homes; assisted living communities with widely different models and levels of services; nursing homes; and the hybrid continuum-of-care retirement communities.

The smaller, private mom-and-pop residences usually have five to six residents and are often located in a converted private home. The owners or managers can be quite good—and sometimes not so good— but the training and level of care may be unsophisticated. Sometimes staff sleeps at night so it's possible for a resident to have falls from bed or other problems that won't be checked or discovered until morning. These homes can be very convenient and affordable, and there may or may not be a lot of understanding, but the expertise will definitely be limited.

The assisted living model requires that staff members are licensed and that someone will be "on their feet" 24 hours a day. The quality and style of assisted living communities vary as much as motel and hotel rooms do. You've got the basic Motel 6 model, the high-end Four Seasons model, and everything in between.

Nursing homes refer to facilities' focus on having skilled nursing available 24 hours a day. However, only about 20% of the elderly who are frail need skilled nursing. Most of the care that is needed can be provided in an assisted living or mom-and-pop community. Help with daily living such as bathing, medications, eating, and general support do not require skilled nursing. A skilled nursing facility is needed for residents with complicated conditions, for example, a patient who is on dialysis, recovering from surgery, and dealing with other serious situations.

Recent years have seen the rise of continuum-of-care retirement communities. These are communities that are designed for active residents by providing them with plenty of opportunity to golf, shop, and engage in social events and other activities; later, they have the option to transition into assisted living, if the need arises. It's important to balance location, convenience, care, oversight, and the proximity of relatives who will be most available for visiting with the type of care and the community that feels right to you and your family. A wonderful community that isn't accessible isn't ideal, nor is a nearby home that feels sad and where residents don't seem loved and valued. Reputation is essential, as are your own observations.

When you begin talking to friends, neighbors, doctors, and local organizations, you'll be amazed at how much expertise there is out there and how much personal experience people have with the different communities. When you begin to take steps, you'll find that a wealth of very helpful information will be made available to you. And you can supplement those recommendations with an inquiry to your local long-term care ombudsman program. The ombudsmen serve as advocates for seniors and their families and regularly visit and monitor care facilities.

Another great resource is your state's licensing agency for assisted living. State inspectors conduct in-person annual inspections of each assisted living community and write up written reports of their findings that you can access.

Costs are a very real concern, but as a close friend and colleague says, "You do not want to negotiate with your heart surgeon." For the most part, higher costs equate to a higher level of service and a higher ratio of staff to residents. On the cost issue, I recommend, to the extent it's possible, to look for the right fit before looking at "cheaper" or "budget" options. You may be surprised at the resources available to you through insurance, savings, Medicare, and Medicaid that can make your community of choice possible. To discuss the financial plan for assisted living, you can meet with the marketing director at the community you're considering and you can get information and guidance through the sign-up process.

All of these essential practical issues aside, the basic advice I give to anyone is to look for love and understanding. It may sound silly, but seek out places where you see people hugging residents. See if the residents appear to be clean and look at their nails, teeth, and clothing. If you visit a place where a resident has food remnants on their clothing or their nails are dirty and untrimmed, you know the care probably isn't what it should be. Visit at both quiet and active times of day, like lunch. You'll see the residents and how they're cared for and how they are treated at meal times. Is spilled food cleaned up? Are the staff members making conversation with the residents, or are they abrupt? Are they loving, and do they address people by their name? Do they know the residents' priorities—for example, their favorite foods, a little bit of their personal history, or a topic they like to discuss? A place may not be beautifully up to date, but if you feel that the residents are receiving caring attention, that is worth a lot. Love and understanding go a long way. The care is incomplete without emotional nurturing.

6. Live with Them in the Disease

When a person has Alzheimer's, a lot of what they do doesn't make sense. We don't "get" how their misfiring brain is creating the different and confusing person in front of us. It's so typical of us as family members to say things like, "Mom, you know your sister died years ago," or "You know Uncle Kenny doesn't live with us anymore." So often, even knowing better, we try to argue with the person who is losing their mind to dementia. This is called "reality therapy," and it is not effective or useful. All it does is agitate the patient. Their brain is telling them that a person is alive.

It used to be that professionals would try to reorient the person to the correct time and place, but we now know this is very harmful because it frustrates the person and leads them to think you are lying to them. With paranoia a part of the constellation of Alzheimer's symptoms, these confrontations over the "truth" play into that tendency. The patient's trust factor goes way down, making everything more challenging.

The important thing to remember is that if you live with the person in their reality, there can be much more harmony and connection. That's why Aegis communities have life-skills stations, where, for example, we display vintage clothes, typewriters, and rotary phones. Many of our communities have "bus stops" where residents can sit on a bench to get "going to work," before their memory lapses and they move on. And our residents love the antique cars we have in some of our community outdoor areas; one, for example, has a 1946 Buick in the parking lot, which brings back so many memories. Some residents view the community car as their own, one they can wash, gas up, and drive, just like they used to, though, of course, the cars don't actually start or go anywhere. These are all examples of ways to accept and live with our loved ones in their reality. It minimizes the agitation and allows for whatever connections that do exist to come forward.

7. Create Familiarity and Comfort

If you were going to move to a 300-square-foot room tomorrow, what are the ten things you'd absolutely miss if you didn't have? It could be a chair or picture you love. Other people want yarn and knitting needles, a musical instrument, photo albums, or books about travel. If someone is religious, a crucifix or a Star of David often gives comfort and connects the person with deep memories from childhood. It is important to make sure that you allow Alzheimer's sufferers to retain whatever items provide them with real joy or passion.

Sometimes the biggest victory is giving the person comfort—especially when we try to celebrate and discover that old traditions like parties or dinners or brunches are too stimulating and stressful. Consider adding decorations to the room that recall great memories, such as a picture of winning an award or a video from a family occasion or certain music that is a reminder of some special time or event—these are all ideal ways to create comfort and familiarity.

With my own mom, for example, because it was very hard for her to put on lace-up shoes, I bought her sock-shoes that were easy to slip on and really warm. She loved them. I bought her several cashmere and silk blankets and other items that felt good on her skin. Especially in the late stages of the disease, these small comforts are all you can do, and they are quite powerful—much more so than you might think.

8. Honor and Celebrate

During the late phases of the disease, traditional ways of celebrating and honoring a person can be overwhelming or simply impossible. Yet honoring the person is so meaningful for us and for them. In our family, we would have family gatherings in my mother's room for birthdays and holidays, sometimes with ten or even twenty people squeezed in. We would reminisce, telling stories like "Mom, remember when we did . . . ? Or "Remember the time we went to Disneyland?" Or "Remember when you broke your foot?" We'd have an actual conversation with her, assuming that she was present and listening, even if she was, emotionally, far away from us in the moment.

There's a tribute aspect to that type of storytelling and there's a residual benefit. It helps the family with closure and is healing in its own right. It speaks to the sufferer's life, to their character, to who they were as a person. Bringing out stories and memories and connecting with other family members in the room all elevate the person beyond their disease. At the darkest hour, this is a very important thing to do. We get beyond seeing just the physicality of the person, who is now ninety-five pounds and weeping. We get beyond watching the decline and crash of a person who at one time took up so much emotional and psychic space in our lives. The person wants to be remembered differently, and we want to remember them differently. When we honor and celebrate and give tribute, we create an opportunity for that to happen.

9. Maximize the Calories

As Americans we want people to eat a certain way. I once wrote a blog about a 92-year-old woman who was eating sugar packets from the table. Her family was horrified and called her doctor to ask what they should do. The doctor's advice? "She's ninety-two. Let her eat the sugar packets!"

Obviously, no one's going to let a resident drink a bottle of bourbon or eat ice cream by the gallon, but in the later stages of the disease, calories become more important than nutrition. The ability to eat declines as the body's functioning declines, and the person just needs nutrition of any type. I would bring my mom carrot cake with icing an inch high, French fries, and other enticing, easy-to-eat goodies. It would provide comfort, familiarity, and calories. You can try to tempt an Alzheimer's patient with special high-nutrient meals of, say, crisp green salad or fresh red beets, but come on! It's not going to happen. Go for the calories. All of you will be happier and—ironically—the patient will probably be healthier.

10. Transport and Connect with Music

Music has incredible therapeutic value. First, there's an almost instinctual physical response. For example, when you put on upbeat music, or a favorite rock and roll song, your body reacts and you start bouncing in your seat, moving your head, and getting a smile on your face. The music physiologically changes your body and attitude. Music itself can construct different moods, and it increases blood circulation. It can be comforting also because music inspires powerful mental associations. Our bodies and hearts "remember," if you will, specific songs, such as a lullaby from childhood or the music played during a couple's first wedding dance.

In my mother's case, we found that music—soft, low in tone, and slow—also helped her to fall asleep at night and sleep longer hours. In the daytime, when we wanted to encourage her presence and alertness, we'd put on her favorite big band music and dance with her. It would often get a big smile out of her and also increased her overall alertness. In every way, music has such a therapeutic value that it's extremely important to make it a part of your loved one's day.

11. Awaken with Nature

It's critical for people with dementia to spend time outdoors, even if they're living in a more urban environment. Unfortunately, people who suffer from Alzheimer's are too often relegated to their rooms or the halls of their community. Anthropologists tell us that we're hard-wired to respond to nature and that there are universal environmental factors that make us feel good, such as water, sun, shade, and natural light. This concept is known as biophilia. When we're cut off from nature we suffer. By contrast, if you undergo surgery and are exposed to natural light through a window (versus a brick wall), your body will heal faster.

Though it's difficult to get them out of their beds or other comfort zones, people with Alzheimer's need to go outside and experience nature's stimuli for healing and comfort—the feel of rain drops, a breeze on the skin, the warmth of the sun, the chirping of birds, the smell of recently cut grass. Even the sounds of children playing or an airplane passing overhead can have a positive effect. These sensations stimulate memories and experiences that make a person feel more whole and alive.

I remember taking my mom out to pick flowers. She always loved the smell, so I put one bud up to her nose and she sniffed it very softly and surprised me with an audible "Ahhh." Even though she wasn't talking a lot, there was some kind of reaction. Her sensory system said, "I like that," as it also did the fresh air and the sun beating on her face. At Aegis, we've even designed clear umbrellas so residents can go outside even if it's raining to get vitamin D, oxygenate their bodies, and still enjoy and experience all the sights and sensory pleasures of the great outdoors.

12. Give the Gift of Touch

Touch is an incredible healing mechanism, so we can't forget to touch the person with Alzheimer's, in spite of their bad breath, messy eating, and lack of responsiveness. More than that, we need a specialized plan to incorporate touch into their lives. Touch is a primal need, as classic studies and Dr. Ashley Montagu's pioneering work showed more than 25 years ago. Without touch, research shows, people and animals fail to thrive. Touch comes in many forms and can fill the void of lost relationships. There is massage, Reiki, and healing touch.

At Aegis, we've had success with reflexology because sometimes a traditional massage can irritate an elderly person's fragile skin and even cause it to tear. Reflexology actually stimulates vital organs and parts of the body through touch of the feet and hands. A wonderful way to experience the power of touch is with a gentle scalp massage during a hair shampoo.

Pets can also provide a healing touch and intimacy. My mom thought dogs had their place—as long as it was away from her—until she was 75 years old, and then all of a sudden she loved dogs. They were on her lap and kissing her and giving her something she physically needed. So touch is a major element that can provide comfort, care, understanding, and stimulation. Discover ways to bring touch into your loved one's life, and it will ease both of you enormously.

13. Always Remember Dignity

One thing I want this book to promote is that every person deserves dignity. We may lose our cognitive functioning and our personality may change, but we don't lose our humanity. Even though a person with Alzheimer's is stuck in their private world, disconnected in many ways from their loved ones, we shouldn't take away their dignity.

That sense of dignity can manifest in a variety of ways. For instance, my mom would never go out of the house without her hair fixed and lipstick applied. So even when she was bedridden, we made sure her hair, face, and nails were done. My mom was always a snazzy dresser, so even at the end, we tried to keep nice, clean, presentable clothes on her. Another woman may have never cared about makeup or clothes but would find it degrading to be bathed by a male nurse; let your care community know and make sure they are following your instructions.

You are displaying real honor toward a loved one and helping them retain their dignity when you do for them what they would want to do for themselves and in the way they would want those things done. We can measure ourselves and the care we're giving and providing by the honor and respect our family members are shown. Dignity, even in the end, is worth so much.

14. Get Care for Yourself and Others

Family members often fall into caretaking roles depending on their inherent personalities, the quality of their relationship with the person with Alzheimer's, and practical issues like work, family, and location. The caregiver who takes on the multitude of daily responsibilities is a heroic person. According to dementia expert Teepa Snow, caregiving is not an option for everyone—it's not something you may feel equipped to do or equipped to do for a particular person (which was the case for Snow's own mother when her grandfather developed Alzheimer's during her childhood). You have to be able to live with and accept the person's reality and allow it to be.

Even the most giving, skilled, and loving family caregiver can get overwhelmed. To be an effective caregiver, you have to start with caring for yourself—you need to know when your trouble light is about to go on and say WARNING, TAKE A BREAK. Caregiver burnout has become rampant in today's society, as people who are compelled by their desire to be a great caregiver usually don't give into their own needs. The end result is bad. The caregiver's physical and mental health condition deteriorates; the person receiving the care also ends up getting substandard care because the caregiver doesn't have the resources to do a good job. So watch for the warning signs: Are you tired, not getting enough sleep, or being awakened in the middle of the night to do care duties? Do you find yourself irritable and getting angry and resentful with the person you are caring for? Are you having trouble completing normal tasks, like cooking, shopping, or doing household chores? If so, your warning light is flashing brightly.

The most important thing you must do for yourself is to make sure you get sleep. If your sleep is frequently interrupted by demands from your loved one or from your own piled-up work, personal needs, or worry, you may need to get help. Home health care agencies can provide nighttime caregivers. Some local government agencies can provide assistance if you don't have the funds. Other resources are local assisted living communities that often offer respite-stay programs. Take a break, even for a week, and move the person you are caring for to a respite program just so you can get a physical and mental rest and recharge your batteries. Do this as often as you need to. There is no guilt in trying to take care of yourself.

We all have to accept that we are mortal, that we have needs, and that in the end we can't help others if we don't also help ourselves. Perhaps we all need to be reminded of the lesson I learned making potato soup with my mother, about being gentle with ourselves and with others. We may think we can do and do and do. We may believe we have somehow failed if we haven't done enough, when there isn't "enough" for a person with Alzheimer's. We may need to remember—over and over again—to be kind to each other. We are all doing the best we can.

Chapter 13

Looking to the Future

by Nora Super

Nora Super has more than 20 years of experience working in Washington, DC, on a wide range of aging policy issues, including health care delivery and payment reform, Medicare, Medicaid, long-term care, retirement income security, and other federal and state aging programs. In her role as chief of programming and services for the National Association of Area Agencies on Aging, she leads all training, technical assistance, research, and development. Previously, Nora served as the executive director of the 2015 White House Conference on Aging, where she was responsible for directing a nationwide effort to identify and advance actions to improve the quality of life of older Americans and issued a report which provides the basis for this chapter.

The White House has announced an extraordinary number of new government actions and initiatives to improve the quality of life of older Americans and their families. At the same time, the private sector has announced a wide range of initiatives to support the same objectives. These initiatives help ensure that Americans have increased opportunity and ability to retire with dignity; that older adults can enjoy the fullest physical, mental, and social well-being; that older adults can maximize their independence and ability to choose to age in place with assistance from caregivers who have the support they need; and that elder abuse—like financial exploitation—is more fully recognized as a serious challenge and addressed accordingly and effectively.

It is time to look to the future to ensure older Americans, and all Americans, will enjoy longer and better lives in the coming decades.

Demographic Changes in Caregiving

First, we must acknowledge our demographic reality.

The United States continues to experience incredible transformation. **Over 10,000 baby boomers are turning 65 every day, and the fastest growing demographic in the United States is women over age 85.**

Most help for older Americans is generally provided at home by non-paid caregivers, especially family and friends. These caregivers are the most familiar face of caregiving, and are often the primary lifeline, safety net, and support system for older adults. As the demographic trends described above accelerate, this reliance will continue to shift to paid caregivers. Accordingly, the conference included much discussion of the policies we need to ensure that we attract and retain a sufficient number of paid caregivers in the profession.

This age wave is expected to continue well into the next century. The population age 65 and over has increased from 35.9 million in 2003 to 44.7 million in 2013 (a 24.7% increase) and is projected to more than double to 98 million in 2060. By 2040, there will be about 82.3 million older persons, over twice their number in 2000. People 65 and older represented 14.1% of the population in the year 2013 but are expected to grow to be 21.7% of the population by 2040. The 85+ population is projected to triple from 6 million in 2013 to 14.6 million in 2040.

Racial and ethnic minority populations have increased from 6.3 million in 2003 (17.5% of the older adult population) to 9.5 million in 2013 (21.2% of older adults) and are projected to increase to 21.1 million in 2030 (28.5% of older adults). Between 2013 and 2030, the white (non-Hispanic) population 65 and older is projected to increase by 50% compared with 123% for other racial and ethnic minority populations, including Hispanics (153%), African-Americans (non-Hispanic) (99%), American Indian and Native Alaskans (non-Hispanic) (104%), and Asians (non-Hispanic) (121%).

To help every American enjoy a longer, better, more active and independent life, society needs to effectively engage the challenges and fully embrace the possibilities inherent in a rapidly aging population. To respond to this challenge over the next decade, both the public and private sectors can examine core societal systems—including work and retirement, health care, housing, and transportation—and how they can better meet the needs of and expand opportunities for a diverse aging population.

Almost 18 million Americans currently provide care for a chronically ill, disabled, or aged family member or friend during any given year. Although non-paid caregivers are diverse in terms of demographic, socio-economic, and cultural characteristics, on average they are more likely to be women (62%) and middle-aged (50% are between 45–64 years).

Caregivers are frequently so engaged in the care of the person they are helping that their own health may not be a top priority. Due to financial or time constraints, these caregivers may go without health care, and ignore the myriad of physical and mental health concerns they often face. They also may sacrifice their own retirement security by leaving employment or reducing work hours in order to care for a family member or friend.

Caregivers provide an average of 75 hours of support per month, but there is great variability depending on the number of caregivers and the older person's level of need. More than half (54%) of caregivers spend more than 40 hours per week providing care to their loved ones. Almost two-thirds of people age 65 and older rely exclusively on informal care for their personal care needs. An additional 30% use a mix of both paid and unpaid care.

The Need for Collaboration

Participants at White House Council on Aging (WHCOA) events have traditionally focused on the need to break down the silos between housing, transportation, health care, and long-term services and supports in order to support healthy aging. Building upon our work at the federal level, we must also leverage the important activities occurring at the state and local levels. Numerous cities and communities have come together to address aging issues with a multifaceted, multidisciplinary approach. These communities are challenging all sectors to re-imagine aging and consider how best to serve and benefit from this growing population. They recognize that healthy aging needs to take place in communities where older adults can be active, where they can find affordable and appropriate housing, and where they can access needed health and social services.

Although rewarding, caregiving can be demanding, and informal caregivers need to be supported and sustained. Informal caregivers also complement the dedicated professional workforce of paid caregivers, who have their own employment, health, and retirement needs, and who continually provide vital support to older Americans.

A growing demand for paid caregivers is expected, which raises issues of recruiting and retaining the direct care workforce. Direct care is a demanding profession with low wages, long hours, and limited benefits. Increasing wages and other measures that improve labor standards for direct care workers are critical to efforts to recruit and retain a sufficient number into the profession to keep pace with the growing need. To address these issues, the Department of Labor issued a final rule to extend federal minimum wage and overtime protections to many home care workers, who, unlike workers who provide services in nursing homes and residential facilities, lacked stronger protections under the Department's prior regulations. More will need to be done in order to ensure that the profession continues to grow and attract the dedicated and skilled caregivers necessary to meet growing needs.

Technology and Aging

In the twenty-first century, technology has transformed what it means to age in America. An increasing array of web-based technologies, robotics, and mobile devices help older adults access the services they need, stay connected to family and friends, and remain active and independent. Unfortunately, technology can also make some older adults more vulnerable to financial exploitation as scammers become more and more sophisticated in how they target victims.

Changing Perceptions

This vision recognizes the possibilities, rather than the problems of aging, and appreciates that older adults have enormous reservoirs of experience and expertise that can make a tangible difference and contribution.

Changing the perception of aging is our ultimate challenge and charge as we go forward into the next decade. By changing Americans' attitudes about aging, we can help every American enjoy a longer, better, more active, and more independent life, and effectively engage the challenges and embrace the possibilities that are inherent in our aging population.

Advances in science and technology hold much promise for helping older Americans remain healthy and prepare for their future, while also helping family and friends support older Americans and avoid financial and other scams. For example, technology may help older Americans to exercise, take medication on time, eat healthy meals, remain safe at home, and connect with family and friends. It can also make it easier for them to travel, find volunteer/employment opportunities, prevent financial exploitation, and live independently in their homes. Advances in the neurosciences of memory and cognition may lead to engaging games and smartphone apps that may demonstrate a role in preventing or slowing cognitive decline.

Conclusion

A half-century ago, before the advent of critical programs, including Medicare and Medicaid and the programs outlined in the Older Americans Act, growing older in America was often synonymous with illness, isolation, and inactivity. The "second half of life" was not necessarily a time to enjoy, but to endure. That is no longer the case. These programs, along with Social Security, provide a foundation of financial and health security to nearly all older Americans. Still, as we move forward, we have much to do.

A diverse citizenry is one of our nation's greatest assets. Communities and populations across the spectrum of ages contribute unique skills, perspectives, and cultures that shape our society. Ensuring that Americans of all ages—including older Americans—are able to contribute to their communities is a role not only for the federal government, but also for the private sector, philanthropists, colleges and universities, professional societies, non-governmental organizations, and state, local, and tribal governments.

Moving forward, we need to appreciate our demographic changes, collaborate across sectors, focus renewed efforts on paid and unpaid caregiving, and, most importantly, foster a cultural change in Americans' attitudes about aging. In doing so, we can help every individual enjoy a longer, better, more active, and more independent life. We need to effectively engage the challenges and embrace the possibilities that are inherent in a rapidly aging population and ensure that all Americans can better age well and live well. Contributing to our society and communities in a meaningful way—that will be the new definition of aging in America as we go forward.

Chapter 14

Your Checklist of Action Items

by Thomas Lee Wright

As you strive to prevent the abuse of your loved one during their advanced years by third parties it's essential to create a simple list of actions to accomplish in order to ensure their safety. In this way, you can take a thorough, methodical approach in your preparations on their behalf.

1. If possible, keep your parents **geographically close**.

2. If you do not live near them, **visit your parents** often.

3. Stay in regular **phone** contact by calling often.

4. Find a doctor you trust and establish through standard testing **a baseline of mental acuity**. In this way you can stay engaged and track any possible deterioration of intellectual functioning.

5. Do **background checks** on any workers who regularly come into contact with your parents.

6. Make note of any **fresh faces or new relationships** that arise in conversation with your parents.

7. Dysfunctional families are easy targets for predatory professionals who regularly take advantage of elders. Always **resolve differences** with your siblings or other family members as quickly as possible. Otherwise, outsiders with bad intentions may try to exploit the discord.

8. Do not allow outsiders to drive a wedge between you and other family members. Always **maintain a unified family front** in the presence of others.

9. Discuss any **family differences** in private.

10. When you receive a gift from a parent who has memory issues, make sure to **document its purpose** in order to share its meaning in the future. For example, a cash loan is almost never intended to be a birthday gift.

11. **Always be present** when your parents are signing any legal document.

12. Always **accompany** your parents on visits **to the doctor**.

13. Make sure the physician has a copy of your **medical power of attorney**.

14. Always ask for copies of the **physician's notes** after any appointment. Avoid **polypharmacy** (overdosing, contraindications, etc.) by monitoring your loved one's use of drugs and doing routine audits of all their prescriptions.

15. Remember to **keep good notes** about your parent's health and well-being—they may become of life and death importance at some point. After your parents are gone, you may not be granted access to any of their health records because of HIPAA laws.

16. Get **regular medical checkups** yourself. Investigate potential hereditary diseases and problematic genetic markers.

17. Assemble a trustworthy **team of professionals** for drafting estate documents comprising a good estate-planning attorney, a licensed financial advisor, a certified public accountant and an honest reliable friend.

18. Always be open to **opposing viewpoints.**

19. **Share with your children** all that you have learned about how to properly protect and care for a loved one because one day they will want to know how best to take care of you.

About the Author

Author and filmmaker **Thomas Lee Wright** has made documentaries for the Discovery Channel and Human Rights Watch, among others. Most recently he directed *Hidden Epidemic: America's Elder Abuse Crisis* and produced *Edith + Eddie,* a star-crossed love story about interracial newlyweds at ages ninety-five and ninety-six. He has appeared on BBC, CNN, PBS, the *Today* show, and other media programs to discuss his work on such topics as prison reform, urban gangs, free speech, international trade, presidential elections, race relations, and the entertainment industry. He is an honors graduate of Harvard University.

Acknowledgments

I would like to thank the following people for their contributions along the journey of this book: Li Ravicz whose wisdom lit the path from grief to action. Mark Gompertz and Joseph Craig who saw the potential and provided patient guidance. Michael Adler, for his friendship and legal advice. Christopher Taylor, intrepid colleague and collaborator. David Steen Martin, investigative reporter extraordinaire. Dwayne Clark, who has made his life's work improving the lives of others. Brett Bowker, historian and researcher. An elite team of crusaders who never stop questing for what's right—Rick and Terri Black, Dr. Sam Sugar, Laura Checkoway, Tom Coleman, Linda and Richard Kincaid. My supportive pals Ciolino, Colker, and the Durtschi family. My father's sister Bev and all the Brunelle nation. My dauntless mother, Beverly, who has faithfully attended the births of all her grandchildren. My sisters Lisa and Kathleen, fellow fighters in the cause. My brother Dan, who is and always has been the very heart of our family. My children, Matthew and Sara Lynne, for their insights and compassion. And fondest thanks to my forty-year partner and better half by far, Alexandra. Lastly, to all those families who've suffered from the scourge of elder abuse, thank you for your courage in sharing your stories and best advice.

Bibliographic Notes

Introduction
Marie-Therese Connelly. Bonnie Brandl, and Risa Breckman. *The Elder Justice Roadmap*, funded by US Department of Justice with support from US Department of Health and Human Services.

Chapter 1
Sarah Jamila Stevenson. "Twenty Facts About Elder Isolation," *A Place for Mom* blog, October 2014.

Chapter 2
Linda Kincaid, original article.

California Assembly Bill 937 (Wieckowski, 2013). Amended CA Probate Code 2531.

California Civil Codes on Elder Abuse. Welfare and Institutions Code 15610.03.

California Civil Codes on Elder Abuse. Welfare and Institutions Code 87468(a)(11)

Chapter 3
Page Ulrey, written testimony, February 2, 2015, US Senate Special Committee on Aging.

Chapter 4

Securities and Exchange Commission's Office of Investor Education and Advocacy and the Consumer Financial Protection Bureau's Office for Older Americans.

Chapter 5

Senator Susan Collins and Senator Clare McCaskill, "Fighting Fraud: U.S. Senate Aging Committee Identifies Top 10 Scams Targeting Our Nation's Seniors," United States Senate Special Committee on Aging pamphlet (October 2015), 1–44.

Chapter 6

Tom Coleman, "The Forgotten Ones," documentary transcript, October 2016.

Chapter 7

The Litigation Limited Guide to Law Firm Overbilling by Litigation Limited, 2012.

Chapter 8

Rick Black and Dr. Sam Sugar, original article.

Chapter 9

Tom Coleman, "Something That's Actually Rigged," *Los Angeles Daily Journal,* November 23, 2016.

Chapter 10

Christopher Taylor, original article.

Chapter 11

David Steen Martin, original article.

Chapter 12

Dwayne Clark, "My Mother, My Son—Part 6: What I Learned: Advice for the Journey," *Aegis Living Publishing* (2012):265–291.

Chapter 13

Nora Super, "2015 White House Council on Aging—Final Report—Executive Summary."

Chapter 14

Thomas Lee Wright, original article.

Index

Treasury Inspector General for Tax Administration, 51
trusts, 30, 44–48, 58, 69, 78, 81, 82, 90, 96, 131

unethical, 92, 93

videotaping, 112, 116
Voice over Internet Protocol, 56
VoIP (Voice over Internet Protocol), 56

United States Senate, 29
Violation, 18, 19–21, 56, 94, 102, 104
visitation, 12, 13, 14, 20–21
vulnerable, 5, 26, 42, 66, 67, 83, 91, 93, 101, 152

warning signs, 26–29, 124, 157
White House, 148, 151
wills, 30, 90, 96